JM

CASEBOOK SERIES

JANE AUSTEN: *Emma* (Revised) David Lodge
JANE AUSTEN: *'Northanger Abbey'* & *'Persuasion'* B. C. Southam
JANE AUSTEN: *'Sense and Sensibility', 'Pride and Prejudice' & 'Mansfield Park'*

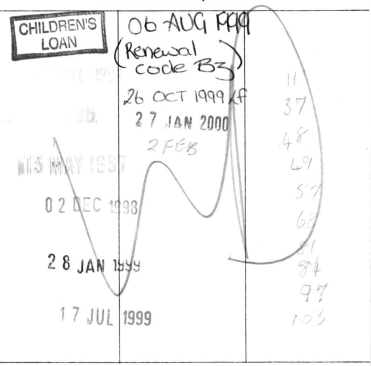

SHAKESPEARE: *Early Tragedies* Neil Taylor & Bryan Loughrey
SHAKESPEARE: *Hamlet* John Jump
SHAKESPEARE: *Henry IV Parts I and II* G.K. Hunter
SHAKESPEARE: *Henry V* Michael Quinn
SHAKESPEARE: *Julius Caesar* Peter Ure
SHAKESPEARE: *King Lear* (Revised) Frank Kermode
SHAKESPEARE: *Macbeth* (Revised) John Wain
SHAKESPEARE: *Measure for Measure* C. K. Stead
SHAKESPEARE: *The Merchant of Venice* John Wilders
SHAKESPEARE: *'Much Ado About Nothing' & 'As You Like It'* John Russell Brown
SHAKESPEARE: *Othello* (Revised) John Wain
SHAKESPEARE: *Richard II* Nicholas Brooke
SHAKESPEARE: *The Sonnets* Peter Jones
SHAKESPEARE: *The Tempest* (Revised) D. J. Palmer
SHAKESPEARE: *Troilus and Cressida* Priscilla Martin
SHAKESPEARE: *Twelfth Night* D. J. Palmer
SHAKESPEARE: *The Winter's Tale* Kenneth Muir
SPENSER: *The Faerie Queene* Peter Bayley
SHERIDAN: *Comedies* Peter Davison
STOPPARD: *'Rosencrantz and Guildenstern are Dead', 'Jumpers' & 'Travesties'* T. Bareham
SWIFT: *Gulliver's Travels* Richard Gravil
SYNGE: *Four Plays* Ronald Ayling
TENNYSON: *In Memoriam* John Dixon Hunt
THACKERAY: *Vanity Fair* Arthur Pollard
TROLLOPE: *The Barsetshire Novels* T. Bareham
WEBSTER: *'The White Devil' & 'The Duchess of Malfi'* R. V. Holdsworth
WILDE: *Comedies* William Tydeman
VIRGINIA WOOLF: *To the Lighthouse* Morris Beja
WORDSWORTH: *Lyrical Ballads* Alun R. Jones & William Tydeman
WORDSWORTH: *The 1807 Poems* Alun R. Jones
WORDSWORTH: *The Prelude* W. J. Harvey & Richard Gravil
YEATS: *Poems 1919–35* Elizabeth Cullingford
YEATS: *Last Poems* Jon Stallworthy

Issues in Contemporary Critical Theory Peter Barry
Thirties Poets: 'The Auden Group' Ronald Carter
Tragedy: Developments in Criticism R.P. Draper
The Epic Ronald Draper
Poetry Criticism and Practice: Developments since the Symbolists A.E. Dyson
Three Contemporary Poets: Gunn, Hughes, Thomas A.E. Dyson
Elizabethan Poetry: Lyrical & Narrative Gerald Hammond
The Metaphysical Poets Gerald Hammond
Medieval English Drama Peter Happé
The English Novel: Developments in Criticism since Henry James Stephen Hazell
Poetry of the First World War Dominic Hibberd
The Romantic Imagination John Spencer Hill
Drama Criticism: Developments since Ibsen Arnold P. Hinchliffe
Three Jacobean Revenge Tragedies R.V. Holdsworth
The Pastoral Mode Bryan Loughrey
The Language of Literature Norman Page
Comedy: Developments in Criticism D.J. Palmer
Studying Shakespeare John Russell Brown
The Gothic Novel Victor Sage
Pre-Romantic Poetry J.R. Watson

William Golding

Novels, 1954–67

Lord of the Flies
The Inheritors
Pincher Martin
Free Fall
The Spire
The Pyramid

A CASEBOOK

EDITED BY

NORMAN PAGE

MACMILLAN

First published 1985 by
THE MACMILLAN PRESS LTD
Houndmills, Basingstoke, Hampshire RG21 2XS
and London
Companies and representatives
throughout the world

ISBN 0–333–37660–9 hardcover
ISBN 0–333–37661–7 paperback

A catalogue record for this book is available
from the British Library

Printed in Hong Kong

12 11 10 9 8 7 6 5 4
03 02 01 00 99 98 97 96 95

CONTENTS

General Editor's Preface   7
Introduction   8

Part One: *Golding and the Reviewers*
A Survey of Responses and Reactions   21

Part Two: *General Discussions of the Novels*
JOHN PETER: The Fables of William Golding   (1957)   33
V. S. PRITCHETT: Pain and William Golding   (1958)   46
FRANK KERMODE: 'Golding's Intellectual Economy'
   (1962)   50
JAMES GINDIN: 'Gimmick' and Metaphor in the
   Novels of William Golding   (1960)   66
PETER GREEN: The World of William Golding   (1963)   76
SAMUEL HYNES: 'Moral Models'   (1976)   97
NORMAN PAGE: Golding's Sources   (1985)   101

Part Three: *Studies on Individual Novels*
C. B. COX: On *Lord of the Flies*   (1960)   115
MARK KINKEAD-WEEKES & IAN GREGOR: 'Approaches
   to *The Inheritors*'   (1967)   122
SAMUEL HYNES: On *Pincher Martin*   (1976)   125
SYLVÈRE MONOD: Golding's View of the Human
   Condition in *Free Fall*   (1982)   133
FRANK KERMODE: On *The Spire*   (1964)   146
DAVID SKILTON: On *The Spire*   (1969)   151
AVRIL HENRY   'Time in *The Pyramid*'   (1969)   166
DAVID SKILTON: *The Pyramid* and Comic Social
   Fiction   (1978)   173

Select Bibliography   184
Notes on Contributors   185
Acknowledgements   187
Index   188

GENERAL EDITOR'S PREFACE

The Casebook series, launched in 1968, has become a well-regarded library of critical studies. The central concern of the series remains the 'single-author' volume, but suggestions from the academic community have led to an extension of the original plan, to include occasional volumes on such general themes as literary 'schools' and genres.

Each volume in the central category deals either with one well-known and influential work by an individual author, or with closely related works by one writer. The main section consists of critical readings, mostly modern, collected from books and journals. A selection of reviews and comments by the author's contemporaries is also included, and sometimes comment from the author himself. The Editor's Introduction charts the reputation of the work or works from the first appearance to the present time.

Volumes in the 'general themes' category are variable in structure but follow the basic purpose of the series in presenting an integrated selection of readings, with an Introduction which explores the theme and discusses the literary and critical issues involved.

A single volume can represent no more than a small selection of critical opinions. Some critics are excluded for reasons of space, and it is hoped that readers will pursue the suggestions for further reading in the Select Bibliography. Other contributions are severed from their original context, to which some readers may wish to turn. Indeed, if they take a hint from the critics represented here, they certainly will.

A. E. DYSON

INTRODUCTION

William Golding was born in Cornwall in 1911. He was educated at Marlborough Grammar School and Brasenose College, Oxford, where he read first science and then English. After leaving Oxford, he spent some time working in the theatre (an experience reflected in *Pincher Martin* and *The Pyramid*), and also published his first book: a slim volume of poems of which he has said that he would 'rather forget it'.[1] In 1939 he married and became a schoolmaster at Bishop Wordsworth's School, Salisbury; but his teaching career was soon interrupted by the outbreak of war. Joining the Royal Navy, he served throughout almost the whole of the Second World War, saw action that included the D-Day landings, and rose to the rank of lieutenant. This period of his life was, again, drawn on in writing *Pincher Martin*.

After the war he returned to his teaching post in Salisbury, and he has lived in Wiltshire ever since. In his spare time he wrote several novels which no publisher would accept; by his own account they were highly derivative – he was imitating the authors he admired in the process of working his way towards an individual style. At last, in 1954, *Lord of the Flies* appeared (1955 in the United States) and was a modest initial success. It was quickly followed by *The Inheritors* (1955; 1962 in USA) and *Pincher Martin* (1956; 1957 in USA), and after a short interval by *Free Fall* (1959; 1960 in USA).

As Part One below indicates ('Golding and the Reviewers'), in a surprisingly short time he had not merely won the respect and admiration of some of his critics but was being regarded as a writer of quite exceptional quality and promise. As early as 1955, one reviewer found in *The Inheritors* evidence of 'his outstanding powers', while in an unusually perceptive review of that novel Isabel Quigley hailed him, on the basis of two short books, as 'the most original and imaginatively exciting' of contemporary novelists (see Part One, below). A couple of years later, another critic, John Peter, concluded a long discussion of his work[*] by declaring that Golding had 'done more for the modern British novel than any of the recent novelists who have emerged'; and soon afterwards a leading British critic, Frank Kermode, saw *Free Fall* as, like Golding's earlier novels, 'a work of genius by a writer . . . in superbly full possession of his great powers'.[*] These are extraordinary tributes (and none the less extraordinary for being richly deserved) to an author whose career had in effect been launched only three or four years earlier. Few writers in any period have received such accolades so early; but then few have produced four major novels in six years. By 1960 it was possible for critics such as Peter Green[*] to undertake a survey of the 'world' of Golding's novels: not only were they the objects of academic attention as well as winning a rapidly increasing general readership, but there was a growing sense that they comprised a body of work that stood apart from the mass of contemporary fiction and had to be judged on its own terms.

An obvious feature of this exceptional career is that Golding began publishing novels relatively late in life. Among his fiction there is no apprentice work, nothing in which we are conscious that he is feeling his way and learning from his failures, as we are in the early novels of, say, Hardy or Lawrence. In *Lord of the Flies* he is already in full command of his art and craft, and it is hard to think of another first novel that moves forward with such sureness and confidence. Part of the explanation, of course, is that it was not a first novel: Golding remarked in a television interview in 1959 that he spent 'ten years, perhaps, learning to write by imitating other people and learning very late that, of course, I was merely writing other people's novels instead of my own'. When, on the same occasion, the interviewer suggested that forty-three was 'rather late to start writing', Golding quickly corrected him: 'I didn't start writing when I was forty; I had been writing ever since I was seven. I suppose you can say I've been effectively writing since I was thirty-

---

* Here and elsewhere in the Introduction, an asterisk within square brackets indicates reference to material included in the Casebook selection below. Numbered references to material or writers cited relate to the Notes at the end of this Introduction.

five.'[2] We may thus compare his case with that of Jane Austen, who published her first novel at thirty-six but had by that time been writing for at least a quarter of a century. Golding added that it was only in about 1948 that he 'grasped the great truth that you've got to write your own books and nobody else's'. No one can say that he has not been doing so, triumphantly, ever since.

Soon his novels began to appear in paperback editions, and there developed the extraordinary rage for *Lord of the Flies*, which quickly became both a campus cult-book and an examination text, and was filmed in 1963. By 1961 Golding was able to retire from teaching to become a full-time writer. *The Spire* followed in 1964 and *The Pyramid* in 1967, and during these years he also published a collection of essays, *The Hot Gates* (1965). Earlier he had written an entertaining play, *The Brass Butterfly*, staged and published in 1958; this is a neo-Shavian comedy of ideas on one of his favourite topics, the place of science and invention in our civilisation.

There followed, unpredictably and for many readers disappointingly, a long silence. Apart from *The Scorpion God* (1971; 1972 in USA), which brings together three stories, Golding published no fiction for twelve years; and since he was by the end of this period nearly seventy years old, some were ready to assume that his career as a writer was over. But Golding has always had the capacity to catch his critics napping, and his silence was broken in 1979 with *Darkness Visible*, which won the James Tait Black Memorial Prize. It was quickly followed by *Rites of Passage* (1980), awarded the Booker McConnell Prize; and *The Paper Men* appeared in 1984. In 1983 Golding was awarded the Nobel Prize for Literature.

This is, evidently, a literary career with more than one unusual feature: his late start as a publishing author, the quick-fire appearance of his early novels, the phenomenal success of his very first novel, the rapidity with which he emerged as a major force to be reckoned with in contemporary literature, the long silence, and the recent appearance of three more novels in six years – all this adds up to a creative record hard to parallel, and probably unique.

Nor is this the only respect in which Golding stands apart

from most other contemporary novelists in Britain. In his very first novel, he cut himself loose at a single stroke from two centuries of tradition in the English novel: centuries during which the realistic mode has been paramount. Golding quickly made it clear that he was interested in a different kind of narrative – one that has been variously referred to as fable, allegory, and myth. What these kinds of narrative have in common is a preoccupation with something that lies beyond that representation or imitation of individual and social realities which has been the bread and butter of novelists from Daniel Defoe to Evelyn Waugh. Golding's concern is with larger, more fundamental and abstract issues that may be called metaphysical or theological. Such works ask not 'How does man live?' but 'What manner of creature is man?' This kind of fiction has celebrated precedents in English – Bunyan's *Pilgrim's Progress*, Swift's *Gulliver's Travels* and Orwell's *Animal Farm* come readily to mind, and Spenser's *Fairie Queene* and Milton's *Paradise Lost* might even be included in this category (a category, it must be quickly added, that accommodates great diversity of purpose and method). But at least since the eighteenth century it has lain at a distance from the mainstream of fictional tradition. Golding's achievement has been to revalidate this alternative tradition for the modern world.

Another contemporary English novelist, Angus Wilson, recognised this when he wrote, in a discussion of 'Evil in the English Novel', that in *Lord of the Flies* Golding 'solved the problem of expressing transcendent good and evil more satisfactorily than any other living English novelist'. For Wilson, however, Golding's early novels remain 'great fables rather than novels'; unorthodoxly, he praises *Free Fall* ('a much better novel than was made out by the critics') because in it Golding had 'shown a need to do what I also believe to be necessary – that is, to wed his sense of a transcendent evil and good to the fully felt social novel that the English have constructed in their great tradition'.[3] I think we can detect here not only Wilson's own commitment, as a practising novelist, to 'the fully felt social novel' (roughly speaking, the nineteenth-century mainstream) but also a kind of uneasiness at the very extent and boldness of Golding's originality and independence.

Wilson would like to see some kind of compromise effected between Golding's fable-making impulse and the 'great tradition' of depicting a world of social relationships. Wilson's is not an isolated voice among Golding's critics, some of whom expressed quite early in his career the wish that he would concern himself more with what he himself has referred to as 'the ordinary universe'[4] – the quotidian and circumstantial, the recognisable world we all inhabit (see, for example, Kingsley Amis's comment in his review of *Pincher Martin*, quoted on p. 25 below).

Golding did not altogether fail to respond to these pleas, and his work has shown fairly progressively, though not without setbacks or backslidings, a preparedness to graft his profound concern with the nature of man on to something that, at least superficially and partially, resembles the social novel of contemporary life. In his first novel, time, place and characters (the future, a tropical island, a group of pre-pubescent boys) had all diverged from normal expectations in the service of a fable of man's nature that also contains elements of parody. His second novel (*The Inheritors*) had plunged into the remote past, taking as its subject Neanderthal man and the coming of homo sapiens, and creating through its remarkable experimental prose the sense of seeing the world not merely through the eyes of other individuals (any good novel does that) but through the eyes and ears and nose of another race of creatures. In his third novel he had appeared to turn to the present day and to a protagonist whose commonplace name seemed to promise realistic treatment (even the title of *Pincher Martin* seems reassuringly traditional); but in the event it turned out to be, in conception and structure, the most daring of Golding's experiments to date – so much so, indeed, that many of the reviewers entirely failed to grasp what was going on, in spite of carefully planted clues and an ending that challenges misinterpretation. It was only in his fourth novel, *Free Fall*, that Golding made concessions to the demand for a more 'normal' kind of novel: concessions that were later made in *The Pyramid, Darkness Visible* and *The Paper Men*, though the concessions, most obviously in the second of these, were far from complete.

As this lightning-survey suggests, variety and unpredictability have been notable features of Golding's career as a novelist. His books have been eagerly awaited, but no one has had the faintest idea what would come next. Who could have foreseen, for instance, that between the relatively realistic *Free Fall* and *The Pyramid* would come (in *The Spire*) a fable about a medieval monk's obsession? Or that the complex *Darkness Visible*, set in the present day, would be followed by a masterly but apparently straightforward piece of historical pastiche in *Rites of Passage*? At the same time, there has been an underlying consistency of purpose, a sense that all these novels, none of which merely repeats or reworks any of the others, are part of a single-minded exploration and exposition of the nature of good and evil.

The problem with such an intention on the part of a novelist – the occupational hazard, as it were, of the fabulist or myth-maker – is that his work may turn out to be too schematic or programmatic, and to present a world so reduced and over-simplified that the reader refuses to grant its authenticity. Such an accusation has been brought against Golding from time to time – for example, by James Gindin:

> . . . the work of one of the most able contemporary fabulists, William Golding, contains a rigid schematisation that tends to force response on the basis of agreement or disagreement with the validity of the author's controlling abstraction. *Lord of the Flies* (1954), by its very form, insists on the recognition of the truth of the orthodox Christian version of essential human depravity: the concept and meaning of the novel rely on the validity of its Christian parallels. Similarly, the whole organisation and direction of *Free Fall* (1959) depends on accepting the relevance of the Faustian bargain, the anguish of selling one's soul to Satan, just as *The Spire* (1964) is dependent on realising the combination of pain and glory in building the monument that aspires to touch the heavens. To question whether the bargain for the soul is applicable to contemporary experience, or to ask if aspiration is really crucially important for man, to wonder about what Satan or the heavens are or even what they might stand for as metaphors, is to destroy the impact of either novel. Golding's novels are so tightly shaped, so intricately structured, that they rest almost entirely on the acceptance of the authenticity of their Christian parallels.[5]

This rigidity, however, may be the outcome of judging Golding's novels by criteria imported from other kinds of fiction. If, for example, we look in *Lord of the Flies* for the kind of presentation of the complexity of human nature and human motives, and the correspondingly subtle discriminations, that we find in George Eliot or Henry James, we shall be sadly disappointed. Ralph, Jack, Piggy, Simon and Roger embody an altogether simpler and starker purpose. But if we regard the story as a fable and discard expectations more appropriate to the realistic novel, we shall find it a remarkable accomplishment. *Lord of the Flies* is closer to such 'moral fables' as *Silas Marner* and *Hard Times*, or such prose allegories as *Heart of Darkness* or the stories of Hawthorne and Melville, than it is to *Middlemarch* or *The Portrait of a Lady*; but it is closer still to the *Pilgrim's Progress* and to a Shakespearean play such as *The Tempest*. Golding's fondness for symbolical and allusive proper names (to cite only one obvious detail) is evidence that he is not primarily concerned with the representation of social or individual realities: his Simon, Nathaniel and Mountjoy, to mention no others, belong to a tradition of naming that includes Miranda and Mr Badman.

One of the characteristics of a Golding novel that marks him out as a writer of rare individuality and power is his use of language. In a period when the style of even gifted and successful novelists seems often afflicted by flatness and banality, Golding has achieved nothing less than a reinvigoration of the English language. It is misleading to talk about Golding's style as if that term denoted a stable set of features, for he has at his disposal a range of linguistic resources that corresponds to the variety of his settings and purposes. The 'style' of *The Inheritors*[6] is quite different from that of *Pincher Martin*, though both books show similar attitudes to language as well as explicit concern with its role in human life.

Golding can penetrate beneath cliché and abstraction, which paralyse so much modern prose, to evoke violent physical sensation so vividly that it seems (such is the power of the illusion) to be unprocessed by the ordering mind, as in the opening passage of *Pincher Martin*:

Then for a moment there was air like a cold mask against his face and he bit into it. Air and water mixed, dragged down into his body like gravel. Muscles, nerves and blood, struggling lungs, a machine in the head, they worked for one moment in an ancient pattern. The lumps of hard water jerked in the gullet, the lips came together and parted, the tongue arched, the brain lit a neon track.

Or, later in the same novel (ch. 3), he can reach beyond sensation:

There was at the centre of all the pictures and pains and voices a fact like a bar of steel, a thing – that which was so nakedly the centre of everything that it could not even examine itself. In the darkness of the skull, it existed, a darker dark, self-existent and indestructible.

Notice how, in these passages, with rare exceptions such as 'self-existent' the words themselves are commonplace. Like some other great writers Golding seems able to accomplish some of his finest effects through words that are commonplace or even clumsy ('lumps of hard water'). Some of Shakespeare's most moving lines consist of words that are in themselves utterly ordinary – Coriolanus's 'There is a world elsewhere', for instance, and Cleopatra's 'Pity me, Charmian, / But do not speak to me'; and among contemporary writers Beckett also has this gift (his short story 'Dante and the Lobster' ends, unforgettably, with the sentence 'It is not', and his trilogy ends 'I can't go on, I'll go on'). Like these writers, Golding seems able to endow words with a special resonance by their placing, by a poetic use of rhythm and cadence, and sometimes by the use of an unremarkable but, in its context, unexpected word, as on the opening page of *The Inheritors*:

Lok's feet were clever. They saw. They threw him round the displayed roots of the beeches, leapt when a puddle of water lay across the trail.

where 'saw' and 'threw' take the reader by surprise.

Golding is quite capable of writing a more self-consciously 'modern' and experimental prose, as in Sammy Mountjoy's first-person recollections of his adolescent emotions in the fourth chapter of *Free Fall*:

They were coming out of the training college already, I could see them, fair heads and mousy ones, giggling and laughing in flocks, tinkling their good-byes and waving so girlish and free, the thin ones, tall ones, dumpy ones, humpy ones, inky ones, slinky ones, gamesy ones and stern ones with glasses on. . . . Had to be accident, I had to be riding when she saw me; so I pushed off and balanced along with circus slowness, half-hoping now that the

crisis was at hand that she would not come out and my misbehaving heart
would be able to settle again, wobble wobble heart and bike and she appeared
with two others, turned and walked away without seeing me.

More characteristic, however, is a less fluent, more strenuous
prose as tough and sharp-edged as a flint tool: phrases such as
'lumps of hard water jerked in the gullet' (in the first quotation
above) exploit the monosyllabic terseness and consonantal
roughness of the language in a way that recalls the poems of
Gerard Manley Hopkins (compare, in *The Wreck of the 'Deutsch-
land'*, 'the sea flint-flake, black-backed in the regular blow').
   Such a prose naturally demands a good deal more from the
reader than the relaxed skimming that is sufficient for much
modern prose: a Golding novel demands to be read as if it were
a long poem, with a willing responsiveness to all the resources
of language. To the question: 'Does this mean that Golding is a
"difficult" writer?' the only answer can be 'Yes and no'. He
certainly does not cultivate obscurity for its own sake: on the
contrary, his intentions are simple, though at the same time
grandly ambitious. He sets out simply (though what could be a
greater subject?) to show us what human beings are really like –
not just as husbands or wives, neighbours or lovers, at work or
in pursuit of happiness (all this being the province of most
fiction), but as souls or essences stripped of all earthly
trappings and seen *sub specie aeternitatis*. From one point of view,
this is a simpler undertaking than that of, say, Trollope or C. P.
Snow laying bare the ramifications and subterfuges of political
life. But comparisons are fruitless, since the very nature of
Golding's interests is entirely different. He is much closer to
such great European novelists as Dostoevski and Kafka than to
most of his predecessors in the English novel. The former, for
instance, gives us in a few sentences of *Crime and Punishment* a
Golding novel in miniature:

   'Where was it', thought Raskolnikov – 'where was it I read about a man
sentenced to death who, one hour before his execution, says or thinks that if he
had to live on some high rock, on a cliff, on a ledge so narrow that there was
only room enough for him to stand there, and if there were bottomless chasms
all round, the ocean, eternal darkness, eternal solitude, and eternal gales, and
if he had to spend all his life on that square yard of space – a thousand years,
an eternity – he'd rather live like that than die at once! . . .'   [ch. 6 of Part II][7]

This nineteenth-century Russian *Pincher Martin* is hard to match in English fiction: preoccupied though they were with death, there is in (for instance) Dickens or Hardy no passage that I know which goes so unerringly to the essence of human existence, as Dostoievski and Golding both do.

Golding has now been publishing novels for thirty years – for all his late start, longer than George Eliot or Hardy, D. H. Lawrence or Virginia Woolf – and many, though not all, would agree that he has lived up to the promise discerned surprisingly early by some of his critics: that he would turn out to be the most original and exciting English novelist of our time. For all the prizes and honours, however, he still has the capacity to surprise and disconcert; and it remains as true as ever that no one can be sure what kind of a novel his next one will be, or what reactions it will elicit. When *Darkness Visible* appeared in 1979, one reviewer found much of it vitiated by 'silliness and tedium' while another deemed it 'one of Golding's finest achievements'.[8] More recently, *The Paper Men* (1984), following hard on the heels of the Nobel award, turned out to be the last thing to be expected from a Grand Old Man of Letters and caused considerable confusion in the critical ranks. One reviewer found it 'trivial', another 'rich as a compost heap' (perhaps an equivocal form of praise), while a third, himself a leading novelist, adopted a wisely cautious stance:

When a piece of fiction seems banal but its author is distinguished and universally honoured, we are compelled to take second and third looks at it, prepared to be convinced that the banality is a kind of code or a new mode of profundity or elegance we are too stupid to perceive.[9]

The brief history of Golding criticism suggests that instant judgements are highly fallible – as, of course, they always have been. *The Pyramid*, for instance, was regarded as an almost naively simple, transparently 'easy' novel by some of its first readers; but subsequent commentators such as Avril Henry [*] and David Skilton [*] have persuasively demonstrated its elaborateness and subtlety. There is no reason to suppose that a major writer's 'codes' can be easily cracked: it is only unimportant writers who fail to challenge, tease, perplex, and sometimes outwit as well as excite their readers and critics.[10]

★

The present volume offers, first, a brief survey of the reception of Golding's first six novels; secondly, a selection of essays discussing his work in general terms or with reference to a group of novels; and thirdly, essays devoted to a single novel. In the third section, *The Spire* and *The Pyramid* are represented a little more heavily than the other novels since for obvious reasons they are left out of account in the earlier surveys of Golding's achievement. The aim has been to represent both earlier and more recent criticism, as well as points of view from both sides of the Atlantic and a variety of critical approaches.

NOTES

1. Bernard F. Dick, ' "The Novelist is a Displaced Person": An Interview with William Golding', *College English*, xxvi (1965), p. 480.

2. Jack I. Biles, *Talk: Conversations with William Golding* (New York, 1970), p. 15.

3. Angus Wilson, 'Evil in the English Novel', *Kenyon Review* xxix (1967), p. 190.

4. Quoted in an essay by Frank Kermode included in this volume (see Part Two below).

5. James Gindin, *Harvest of a Quiet Eye* (Bloomington, Ind., 1971), pp. 341–2.

6. See M. A. K. Halliday, 'Linguistic Function and Literary Style: An Inquiry into the Language of William Golding's *The Inheritors*', in Seymour Chatman (ed.), *Literary Style: A Symposium* (London, 1971).

7. Translation by David Magarshack in the Penguin Classics series (Harmondsworth, 1951), p. 177.

8. Paul Ableman, 'Ignoble Ruin', *Spectator* (13 Oct. 1979), p. 23; Tom Paulin, 'The Fire-Monster', *Encounter* (Jan. 1980), p. 58.

9. Eva Figes, 'All That Glitters', *New Statesman*, (10 Feb. 1984), p. 23; Melvyn Bragg, 'Lord of the Prize', *Punch* (8 Feb. 1984), p. 57; Anthony Burgess, 'A Gesture of Humility', *Observer* (5 Feb. 1984), p. 53.

10. Denis Donoghue has some relevant comments in the fourth of his 1982 Reith Lectures, 'The Cherishing Bureaucracy', *Listener* (2 Dec. 1982), p. 12, where he writes: 'Golding rightly insists that he is not a statue but a moving target: he has other books to write, he is still changing.'

PART ONE

Golding and the Reviewers

A SURVEY OF RESPONSES AND REACTIONS

Any great novel needs to be read more than once – and the second reading will always be a significantly different experience from the first – but Golding's novels imperiously demand it. It is not so much that he is an 'obscure' writer (as Frank Kermode has said, 'despite the roar of baffled critics, Mr Golding's intentions are always simple') as that his is an art of strict economy and total relevance. His novels are short but exceptionally compact and concentrated, with not a word wasted. Not for him the occasional low-pressure passage or sentence that allows the reader's attention momentarily to relax without anything really vital being missed. The poetic strenuousness of his style, like his subtle and complex structural patterns, demand more than most readers are capable of giving on a single reading. Moreover, his fondness for a final reversal that requires everything that has preceded it to be reconsidered in a fresh light means that not even the most perceptive reader is able to grasp the full significance of what he is reading on a first encounter.

A single reading, however, is all that many reviewers in the dailies and weeklies, pressed by deadlines and eyeing their piles of unread books, are willing or perhaps able to give to a new novel; and it should not be surprising, given the conditions of present-day reviewing, that there have been times when appreciation and even comprehension have been lacking. (*Pincher Martin*, as we shall see, offers a notable case in point.) What is striking is how quickly Golding's outstanding quality was recognised by at least some of his critics. When *Lord of the Flies* appeared in 1954, he was unknown as a writer. Although he was in his forties at the time, more than one of his early reviewers referred to him as a promising young author. Its reception was mixed, but it did not go entirely unsung – though no one could have foreseen the unprecedented speed with which it would establish itself as a modern classic and acquire the dignified status of a prescribed text. In the three years 1954–56, reviewers were confronted with three novels, all quite different from each other, and, arguably, each more difficult (or at least more susceptible of misinterpretation) than its predecessor. It is easy to patronise those who, reading in haste and delivering an instant public judgement, fell into error; but it is more useful to consider what qualities struck these first readers most forcibly, rather as it would be valuable to know how first-nighters reacted to *Hamlet* and *King Lear*.

Lord of the Flies   (1954)

The earliest reviews of *Lord of the Flies* appeared on 18 September 1954,[1] and a week later Walter Allen delivered an unfavourable verdict in the *New Statesman*. Conceding that it was 'skilfully told', he found it nevertheless only 'a rather unpleasant and too-easily affecting story'. Much more appreciative was Douglas Hewitt (*Manchester Guardian*, 28 Sept. 1954), who was one of the first critics, if not the very first, to recognise that Golding was a writer of rare quality. Noting that 'It is clear from the start of . . . *Lord of the Flies* . . . that it would be insulting to judge it by any but the most rigorous standard', he finds the book 'completely convincing and often very frightening'. He sums up its weaker side as 'a tendency to be too explicit', and this is perhaps the first rumbling of what was to become a frequent complaint, or at least observation, concerning Golding's work as a whole: that it is often too schematic, and almost diagrammatic, in design and intention. A related point was made by an American reviewer, Louis J. Halle (*Saturday Review*, 15 Oct. 1955), who found evidence that 'the novelist's vision conflicts with that of the textbook anthropologist'. Halle continues:

The novelist sees good opposed to evil; he recognises the existence and the utility of heroes. But the social scientist deals only with amoral phenomena. In his termite society the novelist's heroes are social misfits who must come to a bad end, one suspects, to confirm the tacit assumption that maladjustment is undesirable. The intimidated novelist, thus opposed by the misplaced authority of science, dares hardly suggest even that his heroes save the honour of mankind. The best he can do, at last, is to find a meaningless fulfilment in thrills and horror.

This is not a view of Golding that has stood the test of time: his awareness of good and evil is not inhibited or qualified by the 'authority of science', of which indeed he has a profound distrust.

In the *Listener* (21 Oct. 1954), George D. Painter found it 'a powerful first novel' written 'with style and authority'. The *Times Literary Supplement* on the next day suggested that, though 'fantastic in conception and setting', it 'enlightens and horrifies by its nearness to, rather than its distance from, reality'. John Metcalf (*Spectator*, 1 Oct. 1954) judged it 'a remarkably bitter piece of writing' and hailed its author as a promising younger writer. None of these reviewers can be blamed for failing to predict that within a decade Frank Kermode would be referring to the 'vast readership' of *Lord of the Flies*, which by 1964 had sold over a million copies in the American paperback edition alone,[2] or that in less than that time critics of the stature of E. M. Forster in England and Lionel Trilling in America would be testifying to its quality.[3] Forster speaks of it as 'this remarkable book', while Trilling calls it 'One of the most striking literary phenomena of recent years' and a book that 'seems to have captivated the imagination of a whole generation'. Among works of high literary quality, it is not easy to find parallels to the rapidity with which, after its initial mildly approving reception, *Lord of the Flies* achieved its critical and popular success.

The two novels that quickly followed posed more formidable problems for their reviewers.

The Inheritors (1955)

This novel, though disconcertingly different from most contemporary fiction, did not go altogether unappreciated: G. S. Fraser, for instance, wrote in *Encounter* (Nov. 1955) that, while 'not a novel in the ordinary sense', it represented a great feat of sympathetic imagination'; and the anonymous reviewer in the

Times Literary Supplement (21 Oct. 1955) gave high if qualified praise:

> Even at its most obscure his book has a strange, compelling force and his use of language is vivid and fresh. To bring off what he has tried to do would be an astonishing feat. He has come near enough to it to prove his outstanding powers.

Perhaps the most enthusiastic welcome for *The Inheritors* came from Isabel Quigley (*Spectator*, 30 Sept. 1955), who not only greeted it as a 'many-dimensional and astonishing book' but found evidence in it that Golding 'is the most original and imaginatively exciting novelist we have today' – an extraordinary tribute to a writer who, some twelve months earlier, had been unknown. Isabel Quigley's account of the power of *The Inheritors* is still valid. After pointing out that *Lord of the Flies* was unrepeatable, and that in his new novel Golding 'goes on, and on quite another tack', she writes:

> . . . *The Inheritors* is an enthralling book, enthralling at almost any critical level, its most remarkable achievement as a novel being not so much in the quality of its imagination as in the fact that we are able to share it; that he has harnessed that extraordinary vision to a technique so masterly, a style so taut and accurate and objective, a clarity so bland and therefore so disquieting, as to make us accept it. There is no 'suspension of disbelief' about it, but an active conviction of its truth. Where others have reconstructed a prehistoric past, Mr Golding has created it. You do not think, 'This is marvellously clever'; you think, 'It was so.'

It is true that she fails to see the point of Golding's epigraph from H. G. Wells's *Outline of History*: with hindsight we are in a better position to discern that the intention is ironic and the strategy of using a source negatively a characteristic one of Golding's.

Pincher Martin   (1956)

This next novel proved more recalcitrant: Frank Kermode was later to describe its reception as 'uncomprehending', and Peter Green to make a similar observation in the essay given later in this volume:

> Most critics, with a few honourable exceptions, though they lauded the book

to the skies, completely missed its point. In particular, they objected to what was generally described as the 'trick ending'.

A fair example is Ronald Bryden's review in the *Listener* (29 Nov. 1956). He suggests that Golding's third novel 'proves him . . . a literary artist to be discussed with the utmost seriousness' and that 'he has done memorable justice to his shabby Prometheus, and to his high theme'. But Bryden's account of the story indicates that he has failed to take account either of the ending or of the clues (e.g., the guano, the lobster) that Golding has given the reader along the way:

It is about an ordeal which also is a trial. Flung on a naked scaffold of rock in the Atlantic, his shoddy, desperate hero fights, against a deaf infinity of sea and solitude, the case of his right to survive. Horribly, the prosecuting elements drive his body down the rungs of evolution to the level of the jellies and molluscs which share his toe-hold on existence. Inside, his darting mind, racing against disintegration, scuttles and rummages among the refuse of memory for the evidence of what he has been.

Though an interesting-sounding novel, this is not the novel that Golding wrote. A similar misunderstanding is to be found in Kingsley Amis's review in the *Spectator* (9 Nov. 1956). His summary of Martin's struggles on the rock concludes, '. . . until madness, delirium and (presumably) death overcome him'. Such a misunderstanding invalidates Amis's criticism that, though 'no reader will soon forget the world [the novel] reveals', it lacks universality on account of 'the narrowness and remoteness of that world'. It has been suggested, however, that the novel that followed *Pincher Martin* represents Golding's response to the plea with which Amis ends his review: that he would 'turn his gifts . . . to the world where we have to live'.

Yet another instance of misreading is evident in Hilary Corke's review in *Encounter* (Feb. 1957), which again overlooks the crucial point of Martin's death at the beginning of the book, though it makes a specific issue of begging Golding 'to excise his final sentence in future editions: it cheapens the book and belies its finest values. Besides, that precise particular trick has already been pulled by O. Henry long ago.' That final sentence of the novel caused general puzzlement, and Wayland Young's comments (*Kenyon Review*, Summer 1957) nicely register his own bewilderment:

The ending of *Pincher Martin* is a major puzzle. . . . What exactly has happened? He has somehow got his seaboots back on again. . . . On the level of sheer physical narrative, this is impossible. It is therefore a symbol of the supernatural. Are the seaboots the grace of God? If so, has the whole spell on Rockall been an allegory of purgatory? It may have, and a fine allegory too. But, and here's the rub, we never knew it, and the *lecteur moyen sensuel* can't take the shock of being suddenly told so at the end. This particular trick ending, the trickiest of them all so far, leaves one with a rather rebellious feeling.

No wonder W. J. Harvey felt impelled to remark, somewhat severely, in the following year that the reviews of *Pincher Martin* showed 'just how bad contemporary reviewing can be. . . . Leaving aside the problem of evaluation, one finds a simple inability to understand the novel. . . . *Pincher Martin* is not an easy book but it's not *that* difficult.'[4] Golding's own wry comment on the matter is that he 'fell over backwards in making that novel explicit' and set out to 'write it so vividly and accurately and with such an exact programme that nobody can possibly mistake exactly what I mean' (see Frank Kermode's essay in Part Two, below).

Free Fall   (1959)

If the reception of *Pincher Martin*, according to Professor Kermode, was 'uncomprehending', that of *Free Fall* was 'hostile' – perhaps because that novel is, as he puts it elsewhere, 'reader-repellent'.[5] By this time Golding enjoyed a considerable reputation and the appearance of a new novel by him was a notable event; but disappointment is registered by many of the reviewers of *Free Fall*. Finding it 'something of a disappointment', Goronwy Rees wrote in *Encounter* (Jan. 1960): 'Mr Golding has set himself a problem in metaphysics, and even if we grant, as some do not, the possibility of metaphysics, it is at the very least doubtful whether fiction is the best medium for solving its problems' – to which it may be retorted that a writer as important and as original as Golding is engaged, among other things, in redefining the nature and role of fiction.

Describing it as Golding's 'first social novel', the *Times Literary Supplement* (23 Oct. 1959) also found it 'a disappointment', though adding that 'even poor Golding is better than most other novels published nowadays'. A harsher judgement was delivered by Graham Hough in the *Listener* (5 Nov. 1959). He found Golding's 'moral insights ... not particularly original or striking', and discerned a weakness in the method of the novel: 'the guilt and the corruption are presented largely through introspection; and there is altogether too much of it, and it will not bear the weight it is made to take'. As Hough saw it, in *Free Fall* Golding had turned away from the kind of novel at which, on the evidence of *Lord of the Flies*, he excelled:

I believe the truth is that Mr Golding is at his best as a writer of fable, near-allegory. Complexities of moral judgement are not the main requirement for this kind of writing; it depends on force and vividness in the application of truths that we all know. This was the plane on which *Lord of the Flies* succeeded so powerfully.

Frank Kermode's own verdict (*Spectator*, 23 Oct. 1959) was that the novel 'is not a success': he found 'in the writing a kind of dry heat, a brittleness' and passages where 'for the first time, Mr Golding's invention seems to ebb'. On the other hand, he noted the 'great economy of plot and character. No incident is gratuitous, no character ... can be done without', and concluded that 'one can call the result a failure only if that is a tolerable expression to use of a fiercely distinguished book'.

In a literary career that seemed as compressed and highly-charged as one of his own novels (four books in five years), Golding had already reached the point at which his comparative failures were seen as more interesting than most other men's successes.

The Spire (1964)

Five years later, the interest aroused by *The Spire* can be measured by the sheer volume of reviewing: Professor Biles lists 81 reviews of this novel (and his list is not quite complete) in periodicals that ranged from the *Church Times* to the *Architects' Journal* and the *Oldham Chronicle*. This novel won high, though not unqualified, praise, and we may begin with the comments of three distinguished critics.

In the *New York Review of Books* (30 April 1964; reprinted in *Continuities*, 1968), Frank Kermode, who like others had been 'disappointed' by *Free Fall*, declared that he 'could not imagine a literary event more interesting to me than the publication of the next Golding novel', and in the event found *The Spire* 'a most remarkable book, as unforeseeable as one foresaw, an entire original, yet marked throughout by that peculiar presence. Golding shares with Conrad the habit of writing each new novel as if he had written no other, and certainly no book that had sold a million copies.' His long review (excerpted in this volume, in Part Three) concludes by stressing again Golding's profound originality, his independence from current modes and fashions of fiction: 'It is remote from the mainstream, potent, severe, even forbidding. And in its way it is a marvel.'

Kermode's summing-up of *The Spire* as 'a book about vision and its cost' may be compared with David Lodge's account of it as 'essentially a story of religious *hubris*' (*Spectator*, 10 April 1964). Lodge notes the unifying force of the spire as symbol ('the spire is integral to this theme, lending itself to an astonishing range of metaphorical treatment: it is successively the mast of a ship – the Ark of God, a "diagram of prayer", the phallus of a supine man, a "dunce's cap", a "stone hammer . . . waiting to strike" '), and concludes: '*The Spire* is a superbly written novel, and confirms Mr Golding's claims to be considered as a major novelist. No English novelist of his generation has dared – and achieved – as much.'

In *Encounter* (May 1964), P. N. Furbank, who also had found *Free Fall* 'pretty much of a failure', judged Golding's new novel 'masterly', 'a splendid success, if not an unqualified one – which none of his novels has been since *Lord of the Flies*'. Furbank makes the important point that Golding's prose is a wholly adequate instrument for his vision: 'The prose communicates Jocelin's apocalyptic experience by its impassioned precision of technical detail. And at the high points of technical crisis you see just how masterly this prose, and the narrative handling, can be; for instance, in the great scene in chapter four.' He found the weakness of the novel to lie, 'as so often with Golding, . . . in presenting human relationships' – a point also made in a generally unfavourable review by Richard P.

Brickner (*New Republic*, 23 May 1964), who found it lacking in 'the atmosphere of human behaviour' and concluded that the novel 'does not succeed dramatically – as a novel'. Elizabeth Jennings (*Listener*, 9 April 1964) suggested that not only *The Spire* but Golding's fiction in general is 'totally taken up with one theme – the borderline between reality and madness', and that there is a crucial ambiguity at the heart of the novel: 'one is never absolutely sure whether Jocelin is possessed by a devil or merely mad. . . . He is a tempted visionary, a manic depressive, an obsessive.'

The Pyramid (1967)

By this stage in Golding's career, it had become clear that the only thing that was predictable was his unpredictability; and *The Pyramid*, although seeming to echo *The Spire* in its title, is an entirely different kind of novel – a fact duly noted by its reviewers. As the *Times Literary Supplement* reviewer put it, it 'will astonish by what it is not' (1 June 1967). Whereas most if not all of Golding's novels up to and including *The Spire* had 'expressed a single imagination and a single literary intention of a kind not usual in modern writing', *The Pyramid* disconcertingly broke the pattern of 'common allegorical (or fabulous or mythical) form', and turned out to be 'a low-keyed realistic novel of growing up in a small town – the sort of book H. G. Wells might have written if he had been more attentive to his style'. The analyses of later critics who have been able to examine *The Pyramid* at their leisure indicate that this view of it as a superior latter-day *History of Mr Polly* is seriously inadequate: see, for example, the discussion of its structure by Avril Henry (excerpted in Part Three of this volume) and of its Trollopean echoes by David Skilton (also included in Part Three below).

The Pyramid won high praise from Martin Seymour-Smith (*Spectator*, 30 June 1967), who found it 'a subtle and complex work' and 'Golding's finest novel so far'. . . . Golding is without doubt a master, now perfecting his own way of coping with reality.' While suggesting that the story is 'deceptively ordinary and plotless' but contains hidden depths, Seymour-Smith seems to experience a sense of relief that Golding is giving his readers a more traditional and accessible kind of novel, 'too good to be desiccated by talk of myth, fable, and even allegory; it should be responded to in its own richly human terms'. Another reviewer, Hilary Corke (*Listener*, 8 June 1967), also noted that Golding was now 'in the English novel's central tradition'. While not untrue, these judgements are far from being the whole truth.

It seems that, even after six novels, Golding was capable of setting problems incapable of solution in the normal conditions of book-reviewing – which is saying no more than that, like any great works of literature, his novels demand to be read slowly or at least unhurriedly, reflected on, and re-read before the reader can feel even moderately confident that he is beginning to arrive at an understanding of them. His most recent novels are beyond the scope of this survey or the present volume, but he has not lost his capacity to provoke a variety of judgements; and it will be interesting to see whether, for instance, some of the reviewers who have found little to commend in *The Paper Men* (1984) have occasion to eat their words in a few years' time.

NOTES

1. A useful list of early reviews of Golding's books is included in Jack I. Biles, 'William Golding: Bibliography of Primary and Secondary Sources', in *William Golding: Some Critical Considerations*, ed. Jack I. Biles and Robert O. Evans (Lexington, Ky, 1978), pp. 237–80.
2. Frank Kermode, *Continuities* (London and New York, 1968), p. 186.
3. E. M. Forster, Introduction to *Lord of the Flies* (1962 reprint); Lionel Trilling, '*Lord of the Flies*', in *Mid-Century* (Oct. 1962), pp. 10–12.
4. W. J. Harvey, 'The Reviewing of Contemporary Fiction', *Essays in Criticism*, VIII (1958), p. 185. Harvey's contribution to the debate on the ending of *Pincher Martin* is that Golding 'has mistrusted his own strength, hence the give-away on the last page. This last chapter is a pity; it destroys the unity of the rest without really providing an enveloping ironic frame; the twist in the tail emerges as a cheap gimmick and . . . it doesn't really serve to enlighten the more obtuse of his readers. Compare it with the beautifully-pointed irony of the last paragraph of *Lord of the Flies*, and its superfluity becomes obvious' (pp. 184–5).
5. Kermode, *Continuities*, p. 186.

PART TWO

General Discussions of the Novels

John Peter The Fables of William Golding (1957)

A useful critical distinction may be drawn between a fiction and a fable. Like most worthwhile distinctions it is often easy to detect, less easy to define. The difficulty arises because the clearest definition would be in terms of an author's intentions, his pre-verbal procedures, and these are largely inscrutable and wholly imprecise. For a definition that is objective and specific we are reduced to an 'as if', which is at best clumsy and at worst perhaps delusive.

The distinction itself seems real enough. Fables are those narratives which leave the impression that their purpose was anterior, some initial thesis or contention which they are apparently concerned to embody and express in concrete terms. Fables always give the impression that they were preceded by the conclusion which it is their function to draw, though of course it is doubtful whether any author foresees his conclusions as fully as this, and unlikely that his work would be improved if he did. The effect of a fiction is very different. Here the author's aim, as it appears from what he has written, is evidently to present a more or less faithful reflection of the complexities, and often of the irrelevancies, of life as it is actually experienced. Such conclusions as he may draw – he is under much less compulsion to draw them than a writer of fables – do not appear to be anterior but on the contrary take their origin from the fiction itself, in which they are latent, and occasionally unrecognised. It is a matter of approach, so far as that can be gauged. Fictions make only a limited attempt to generalise and explain the experience with which they deal, since their concern is normally with the uniqueness of this experience. Fables, starting from a skeletal abstract, must flesh out that abstract with the appearances of 'real life' in order to render it interesting and cogent. *1984* is thus an obvious example of a fable, while *The Rainbow* is a fiction. Orwell and Lawrence, in these books, are really moving in opposite directions. If their movements could be geometrically projected, to exaggerate and expose each other, Lawrence's would culminate in chaotic reportage, Orwell's in stark allegory.

The distinction need not be limited to novels. *The Atheist's Tragedy* by Tourneur is a fable, Shakespeare's *Troilus and Cressida* resembles a fiction, and perhaps an analogous (though modified) difference can be detected between *Paradise Lost* and *The Prelude*. Yet it has a particular value for the critic whose concern is with novels, in that it assists him in locating and defining certain merits which are especially characteristic of novels, and certain faults to which they are especially prone. Both types, the fiction and the fable, have their own particular dangers. The danger that threatens a fiction is simply that it will become confused, so richly faithful to the complexity of human existence as to lose all its shape and organisation. This happens in Lawrence's *Kangaroo*, for instance, and perhaps in some of Dostoevsky's work also. My impression is that modern American novelists have often had to contend with this difficulty, not always successfully. The danger that threatens a fable is utterly different, in fact the precise opposite. When a fable is poor – geometrically projected again – it is bare and diagrammatic, insufficiently clothed in its garment of actuality, and in turn its appeal is extra-aesthetic and narrow. Satires like *Animal Farm* are of this kind.

It will be said that any such distinction must be a neutral one, and that the best novels are fictions which have managed to retain their due share of the fable's coherence and order. No doubt this is true. But it also seems to be true that novels can go a good deal farther, without serious damage, in the direction of fiction than they can in the direction of fable, and this suggests that fiction is a much more congenial mode for the novelist than fable can ever be. The trouble with the mode of fable is that it is constricting. As soon as a novelist has a particular end in view the materials from which he may choose begin to shrink, and to dispose themselves toward that end. Readers of *War and Peace* will remember the passage (at the opening of Book VI) where Prince Andrew Bolkónski drives past a bare oak in the forest on his way to visit the Rostóvs, and how on his return the oak has burst into leaf. The technique here approximates to the technique of fable, since the burgeoning of the tree is meant to symbolise his awakening feelings for Natásha, and it is curiously ineffective beside the fictional richness of the rest of the book. Compare it, for instance, with the idyllic account of the Rostóvs' country amusements in Book vii, which serves only a general purpose and is not fettered by pre-existing intentions, and it appears perfunctory and crude. To put it in another way, the old oak seen by Bolkónski is an author's prop, with none of the unpremeditated cogency of the wet birches beside the road down which, in Book ix, Nicholas Rostóv rides to the engagement at Ostróvna. These are barely mentioned, but they are *there*. The fact is that a novelist depends ultimately not only on the richness of his materials but on the richness of his interests too; and fable, by tying these to a specific end, tends to reduce both. Even the most chaotic fiction will have some sort of emergent meaning, provided it is a full and viable reflection of the life from which it derives, if only because the unconscious preoccupations of the novelist will help to impart such meaning to it, drawing it into certain lines like iron filing sprinkled in a magnetic field. Fables, however, can only be submerged in actuality with difficulty, and they are liable to bob up again like corks, in all their plain explicitness. It may even be true to say that they are best embodied in short stories, where economy is vital and 'pointlessness' (except for its brevity) comparatively intolerable.

If this is so, and creative profundity less inaccessible in fiction, why should so many modern authors prefer the mode of fable? For many do, the results ranging from the puerilities of Rex Warner, through average work like Moravia's *The Conformist*, and respectable work like Orwell's, to the significant achievement of Franz Kafka. Part of the answer lies no doubt, in our reluctance to admit that a particular and personal history can be as momentous as a symbolic paradigm. As Alan M. Boase put it some years ago, in introducing a play by Jean Cocteau to the British public: . . .

[Peter here quotes material in French, which we translate:
 'To be moved by fictional characters who lack symbolic value seems more

and more to be an abuse of our capacity for allowing ourselves to feel pity in an age when the atrocity of the destiny of so many real creatures demands our sympathy' – Ed.]

This is shrewdly observed. Nowadays we can only weep for King Lear after reassuring ourselves that he is less a man than Man, for our instinctive approach to Tragedy is quantitative, a matter not of depth but of scale. Then too, besides this, there is a special pragmatism in our approach to literature. We prefer our art applied, not pure, and are impatient with the indirectness of fiction and unsatisfied by the passive enrichment it can provide. The coherence of fable appeals to us as a moral tool, and its patterns become precepts. Much of this reasoning is obtuse, like the anxious student asking his instructor, 'But sir, what is this Shakespeare play *about*?' but it is very prevalent. The upshot is that fable has heavily encroached on fiction in our time. Future critics, looking back, may well conclude that the best work of our generation was done in this mode, a compromise of proselytism and art like the literature of the Middle Ages.

These reflections are the result of a perusal of three books by an English writer, William Golding. Their titles are *Lord of the Flies*, *The Inheritors* and *The Two Deaths of Christopher Martin* (or *Pincher Martin*, as it was called in the English edition). All three are recent, and generally speaking all have been very well received. . . .

It is obvious that [the] conclusion [of *Lord of the Flies*] is not a concession to readers who require a happy ending – only an idiot will suppose that the book ends happily – but a deliberate device by which to throw the story into focus. With the appearance of the naval officer the bloodthirsty hunters are instantly reduced to a group of painted urchins, led by 'a little boy who wore the remains of an extraordinary black cap', yet the reduction cannot expunge the knowledge of what they have done and meant to do. The abrupt return to childhood, to insignificance, underscores the argument of the narrative: that Evil is inherent in the human mind itself, whatever innocence may cloak it, ready to put forth its strength as soon as the occasion is propitious. This is Golding's theme, and it takes on a frightful force by being presented in juvenile terms, in a setting that is twice deliberately likened to the sunny Coral Island of R. M. Ballantyne. The boys' society represents, in embryo, the society of the adult world, their impulses and convictions are those of adults incisively abridged, and the whole narrative is a powerfully ironic commentary on the nature of Man, an accusation levelled at us all. There are no excuses for complacency in the fretful conscientiousness of Ralph, the leader, nor in Piggy's anxious commonsense, nor are the miscreants made to seem exceptional. When he first encounters a pig Jack Merridew is quite incapable of harming it, 'because of the enormity of the knife descending and cutting into living flesh', and even the delinquent Roger is at first restrained by the taboos of 'parents and school and policemen and the law'. Strip these away and even Ralph might be a hunter: it is his duties as a leader that save him, rather than any intrinsic virtue in himself. Like any orthodox moralist Golding insists that Man is a fallen creature, but he refuses to hypostatise Evil or to locate it in a dimension of its own. On the contrary Beëlzebub, Lord of the Flies, is Roger and Jack and you and I, ready to declare himself as soon as we permit him to.

The intentness with which this thesis is developed leaves no doubt that the novel is a fable, a deliberate translation of a proposition into the dramatised terms of art, and as usual we have to ask ourselves how resourceful and complete the translation has been, how fully the thesis has been absorbed and rendered implicit in the tale as it is told. A writer of fables will heat his story at the fire of his convictions, but when he has finished the story must glow apart, generating its own heat from within. Golding himself provides a criterion for judgement here, for he offers a striking example of how complete the translation of a statement into plastic terms can be. Soon after their arrival the children develop an irrational suspicion that there is a predatory beast at large on the island. This has of course no real existence, as Piggy for one points out, but to the littluns it is almost as tangible as their castles in the sand, and most of the older boys are afraid they may be right. One night when all are sleeping there is an air battle ten miles above the sea and a parachuted man, already dead, comes drifting down through the darkness, to settle among the rocks that crown the island's only mountain. There the corpse lies unnoticed, rising and falling with the gusts of the wind, its harness snagged on the bushes and its parachute distending and collapsing. When it is discovered and the frightened boys mistake it for the beast the sequence is natural and convincing, yet the implicit statement is quite unmistakable too. The incomprehensible threat which has hung over them, is, so to speak, identified and explained: a nameless figure who is Man himself, the boys' own natures, the something that all humans have in common.

This is finely done and needs no further comment, but unhappily the explicit comment has already been provided, in Simon's halting explanation of the beast's identity: 'What I mean is . . . maybe it's only us.' And a little later we are told that 'However Simon thought of the beast, there rose before his inward sight the picture of a human at once heroic and sick.' This over-explicitness is my main criticism of what is in many ways a work of real distinction, and for two reasons it appears to be a serious one. In the first place the fault is precisely that which any fable is likely to incur: the incomplete translation of its thesis into its story so that much remains external and extrinsic, the teller's assertion rather than the tale's enactment before our eyes. In the second place the fault is a persistent one, and cannot easily be discounted or ignored. It appears in expository annotations like this, when Ralph and Jack begin to quarrel:

The two boys faced each other. There was the brilliant world of hunting, tactics, fierce exhilaration, skill; and there was the world of longing and baffled commonsense.

Less tolerably, it obtrudes itself in almost everything – thought, action, and hallucination – that concerns the clairvoyant Simon, the 'batty' boy who understands 'mankind's essential illness', who knows that Ralph will get back to where he came from, and who implausibly converses with the Lord of the Flies. Some warrant is provided for this clairvoyance in Simon's mysterious illness, but it is inadequate. The boy remains unconvincing in himself, and his presence constitutes a standing invitation to the author to avoid the trickiest problems of his method, by commenting too baldly on the issues he has raised. Any writer of fables must find it hard to ignore an invitation of this kind once it exists. Golding has not been able to ignore it, and the blemishes that result impose some serious, though not decisive, limitations on a fiery and disturbing story.

The Inheritors, published in 1955, is again an indictment of natural human depravity, though to its author's credit it takes a quite different form. This time the central characters are a group of hairy, simian pre-humans, much like Yahoos in appearance but in other respects very different. The people, as they call themselves, are as intelligent as their experience permits them to be, they are warm-hearted and reverent – quite simply, good – and Golding invests them with a quite extraordinary charm. The group is only a remnant, those who have survived a forest fire, and the story tells of their encounter with other creatures whose existence has hitherto been un-known to them, men and women. Their instinctive reaction to these strangers is one of admiration and affection (it is typical that they should at first regard the poisoned arrows shot at them as gifts), but for their part the humans hate and fear them, killing them on sight. Inevitably they are destroyed. The narrative closes with a last survivor, Lok, in his death-throe, howling his grief for the companions he has lost, for the inexplicable misery that has possessed him, while the humans row away in their dug-out down the lake.

Like its predecessor *The Inheritors* is a disturbing book to read, passionate, often moving, and with a rich command of irony. There is a passage in Sir William Walton's . . . opera, *Troilus and Cressida*, that might stand for irony at its laconic best – when the lovers' duet in gratitude to Aphrodite for having answered their prayer and brought them togeher is immediately and tartly succeeded by Pandarus's theme from the orchestra. Golding's irony seems not a whit inferior when, after one of their number has disappeared, he shows the people's bewilder-ment and anxiety, allows them to take comfort from the thought that the missing Ha will have been befriended by the humans, because 'People understand each other', and appends the sentence: 'The people considered this and shook their heads in agreement.' But this adroitness is not confined to isolated passages. The narrative relies heavily on irony for its pungency, and even the title and the epigraph were clearly chosen for their ironic force. The title reminds us that it was the meek who were to inherit the earth. The epigraph (a passage from Wells' *Outline of History*, suggesting that the ogre of folk-lore may derive from 'the dim racial remembrance' of 'gorilla-like monsters, with cunning brains, shambling gait, hairy bodies, strong teeth, and possibly cannibalistic tendencies') is tellingly reinterpreted in what succeeds, where all doubt as to who are monsters and who not is soon dispelled. The very core of the book is ironic, for its purpose is to play off against our smug prejudices – like those of the epigraph – a representation of their grounds that is as humiliating as it is unexpected. Irony of this kind is always valuable to an author who wishes to be challenging, as Swift knew when he put Gulliver in Brobdignag, but what gives it a special value here is its capacity to function instead of an explanatory commentary. We are sufficiently familiar with the ways of men and women to form an adequate idea of the motives of the humans, but their actions are presented through the eyes of Lok and his companions. Thus a persistent discrepancy is maintained between appearances and realities, and it is across this gap that the sparks of irony can crackle most sharply. No explicit comments are needed, for even an inattentive reader can see what is going on, and how it is being misinterpreted. The effect is that propositions pass quite smoothly into plastic terms, leaving no unnecessary residue to clog the prose.

Golding's skill and assurance can be seen throughout *The Inheritors*, both in this implicit exposition and in the approach he takes, beginning with the people and, by initiating us into their mental processes, establishing their full claim on our sympathy. Only at the end is the viewpoint altered to allow us to identify ourselves with the humans, after seeing Lok from the outside as 'the red creature', and by then of course it is too late. The conclusion has something in common with the last pages of *Lord of the Flies*, when the naval officer makes his appearance, but the effect here is poignant as well as interpretative: Lok sits weeping for Liku, with her doll clasped in his hand, a more pathetic figure than any man could be because of his simplicity. It might be argued that all these effects are built on a basic fallacy, and that if all humans were as slenderly endowed with pity and benevolence as those in the book it would be unintelligible to its readers; but this is only a debater's point, itself fallacious and in any case altogether divorced from any honest response to the story as it is told. Again, a fable so intimately concerned with semi-mythical creatures might easily seem sketchy or incredible. Yet it is sensuously and persuasively rendered and seems unquestionably real. The people's existence is remote from any conception of existence we possess but its physical conditions are carefully re-created, and any thinness in its subjective texture is naturally referred to the limited awareness they enjoy. Since there is no equivalent to the boy Simon, the irony serving to replace him, the book is also more strictly faithful to the canons of its aesthetic type. It seems to me a marked improvement over *Lord of the Flies* and that in itself is no mean praise.

The new novel, which appeared as *Pincher Martin* in 1956, is again a species of fable, though its thesis is much more difficult to infer than those of its predecessors. This obscurity is partly stylistic, the outcome of a prose which has grown progressively cryptic through the three books, but it is also a result of the book's construction, the unprecedented obliquity with which the author's drift appears. Christopher Martin, precariously afloat in the sea after being torpedoed, is able to clamber exhaustedly on to Rockall, the bare tooth of rock in the North Atlantic, and there he keeps himself alive for six days while memory, and in time delirium, gradually gnaw away his consciousness. Unlike Crusoe, he is never rescued. Unlike Crusoe also, he is by human standards despicable. As his memories unfold we learn that he is a vain *poseur*, obsessively selfish, a thief, a cheat in examinations and in personal relationships, an adulterer, a rapist, and (in intention at least) a murderer too. The bleakness of his solitude offers no security against introspection and, as his selfishness comes to comprehend the self it serves, his personality disintegrates. Inexorably, as he has eaten others, the rocky teeth in the sea eat him. He

goes mad and dies during an apocalyptic storm, his vision
tormented by the hallucinations engendered by fever and
self-disgust.

So, at least, the few reviews I have seen maintain. As we have
observed, however, the endings of Golding's books are always
significant, and here a brief final chapter is appended in which
we learn that Martin's body, washed ashore, still wears the
seaboots of which he had divested himself on the fourth page of
the story – a revelation which is all the more portentous for
being reserved until the very last sentence of the book. He has
not been out of the water, whether on Rockall or anywhere else.
What does this extraordinarily belated disclosure involve?

In the case of most of Golding's contemporaries what it
involved would be simple ineptitude. If the plot were what
ostensibly it is, with no rescue and no redeeming features in the
protagonist, it would inevitably tail away into nullity or
infinitude, in effect disappearing below or above the level of
feasible dramatisation, and the last sentence would be a
meretricious attempt to vivify and complicate it, an endeavor
(to adapt Golding's own metaphor for voracity) to eat one's
corpse and have it too. But this novel is on a quite different level
of achievement from *The Flight from the Enchanter*, for example,
and in fact the disclosure about Martin's boots is both crucial
and integrally related to what has gone before. Myself, I found
that it necessitated reading the book again, and only when this
had been done did the subtlety of the design begin to reveal
itself. It is indeed so subtle, being to *Lord of the Flies* and *The
Inheritors* much as symbolism is to allegory, that it cannot be
satisfactorily translated or paraphrased. I attempt some translation here to dispel the false impression which the reviewers
may have given, lest the figure in the carpet – more, the carpet
itself – should go altogether unappreciated.

The essential point is that this is a story about a dead man. It
is about a consciousness so self-centered and so terrified of the
infinite that it creates for itself, even in death, a fantasy
existence which, however arduous and painful, nevertheless
still permits it the luxury of personal identity. Dead as he is,
Martin clings savagely to the idea of survival, inventing a rocky
outcrop on which he can exist, inventing the conditions of that

existence, re-creating his naval identity disc to prove that he is
still himself, continually applying the intellect of which he is so
impiously proud to obliterate and deny the fact of death.

> I won't die.
> I can't die.
> Not me—
> Precious,

he thinks at the outset, and in a sense, for a time, he does not.
But the existence he enjoys is a figment of his own will only, and
in the most secret recesses of his being he remains horrifiedly
aware of its unreality. This is why he is afraid of sleep, with its
surrender of control, and appalled when he discovers that he
has seen a red lobster in the sea, or forgotten that guano is
insoluble. His intellect, commissioned to establish a mode of
life for him, has made mistakes about these details, and the
errors force him to admit, for a searing moment, that his whole
environment is as imaginary as the dissolved guano or the
lobster. I think the ambiguity here is masterly, for at first one
supposes that his fear is simply a fear of insanity. Yet, as later
appears, Martin is not afraid of insanity. He even courts it for
himself, destroying his water-supply and shouting 'Mad! Proof
of madness!' when it is gone. The fact is that when his imagined
existence begins to dissolve there is only one alternative to
death remaining to him, only one last crevice in which he can
hide: either he is dead, or he is insane. So terrified is he of 'the
positive, unquestionable nothingness' that he seizes on the alibi
of insanity to deny it; and already, characteristically, he is
slopping about in self-pity, dramatising himself as a 'Poor mad
sailor on a rock', his fraudulent mummery brilliantly indicated
in the enfeebled lines he misremembers from *King Lear*. When,
towards the end, he creates an image of God dressed as a
mariner, and defies it – 'I have created you and I can create my
own heaven' – the figure replies soberly, 'You have created it.'
He has indeed, out of the resources of his own being, but these
are so utterly impoverished that it cannot endure. The absolute
black lightning of which his friend Nathaniel Walterson had
spoken, the instrument of divine vengeance for all who lack 'the
technique of dying into heaven', comes to annihilate the

theatrical paper world he has made for himself, and he lapses into the death he has repudiated, the compassion (as Golding expresses it) that is timeless and without mercy.

The book seems to me, in all seriousness, as brilliant a conception as any fable in English prose. Perhaps the execution is not absolutely faultless, but it is impressive, with the interest finely sustained through nearly two hundred pages of ambiguity. Yet the novel is more than a technical *tour de force*. It has the organisation of a poem and, like a good poem, its ultimate power lies less in the resources of its parts than in its scope as a whole. The symbols that it uses – black lightning, eating, the Chinese box – may not be uniformly compelling but they are integrated into a pattern which is, a pattern where the meaning is difficult to exhaust. This is where the book differs from its predecessors, in a sense transcending the mode of fable itself. In the earlier books the thesis to be conveyed is comparatively specific: however trenchantly expressed, however sensitively embodied, it remains finite and in consequence limited, what oft was thought but ne'er so well expressed. This one is richer because exploratory, a configuration of symbols rather than an allegory, and for this reason it will bear an intensity of attention that its predecessors could not sustain. Perhaps because it *is* exploratory it lacks a little of the clarity, and more of the warmth, of *The Inheritors*. The alternative to Martin's self-worship has to emerge by negative implication, where the goodness of Lok and the people appeared directly, and the human agents of the fable (Nathaniel and Mr Campbell, though not Pete) sometimes come uncomfortably close to the Simon of *Lord of the Flies*. There is a degree of obscurity too about the symbol of the cellar, representing childhood terror, which seems to me either unnecessary or indicative of a limited but lurking incoherence. And there is some tenuity here and there, the result of conciseness, in the flashes of reality glimpsed in Martin's memories. But these are niggling criticisms. What impresses, beyond the qualification of any minor weakness, is the profundity and power of the emerging pattern, and the assurance that has left it to speak for itself. The book is arresting, with an originality all its own. It is also a penetrating comment on corruptions of consciousness which, however inveterate, are particularly in evidence today – some of them indeed, the less noxious, associated with our preference for fable over fiction.

This brings me back, uneasily, to my original point, that fable tends to tie a writer down within his conscious purposes, restraining him, while the freedom of fiction can draw him out beyond his ascertained abilities. In view of the level of Golding's achievement, especially here, it seems futile to insist that he will never be a major novelist, but the doubt must remain to taunt an admirer like myself. Obviously a man has to write in the vein that suits him best, so that it would be impertinent, and probably destructive, to urge a maker of fables to apply himself to fictions. But it is easy to imagine some critic of the future assessing Golding's case, and deploring the conditions for literature which drove a talent so egregious into the narrow province of fable, instead of enlarging and enriching it. To such a critic a moderate success in the mode of fiction, like Angus Wilson's *Anglo-Saxon Attitudes*, may well seem preferable to any fables contemporary with it, however finely done.

Judgements of this kind are not predictable, however, and in the interim work like Golding's deserves much more than casual praise. I mentioned Walton earlier and am reminded of Sir Donald Tovey's comment on his Viola Concerto, composed when he was a young man of 27: 'This seems to me to be one of the most important modern concertos for any instrument, and I can see no limits to what may be expected of the tone-poet who could create it.' Though the limits are clearer, of Golding something very similar might be said. To have published three such books as these in as many years, to be capable alike of the compassion of *The Inheritors* and the brilliance of *Christopher Martin*, to be able to write with the art and the succinctness that almost every page reveals – capacities of this order, in lean times like ours, inspire something close to awe. Already, working in a recalcitrant mode, he seems to me to have done more for the modern British novel than any of the recent novelists who have emerged. More, it may be, than all of them.

SOURCE: essay (here in slightly shortened form) in *Kenyon Review*, XIX (1957), pp. 577–80, 582–92.

V. S. Pritchett   Pain and William Golding   (1958)

The essence of the novelist's art – especially the English novelist's – is the quotidian. From the moment Crusoe domesticates and diarises his desert island, the novel reflects the confidence the individual derives from the society he lives in. The risks of romance are gone; he is safe in the realists's nest: Selkirk was lonely, but Crusoe is the least lonely man in the world. This confidence has lasted in our tradition. But when we look up from our books into the life around us today, we wonder how the prosaic observer in realistic fiction can be so certain of himself. The quotidian art goes on describing and describing and, as far as externals are concerned, we cannot complain that the modern realist fails to describe the features of a changing, violent or collapsing society. But he is the spectator, in some lucky way insured and untouched; rarely does the novelist find the point at which we are involved or committed; rarely does he touch the quick, so that for once the modern alibi – 'it is beyond the power of the imagination to grasp. etc., etc.' – does not work. The imagination will never grasp until it is awakened; and facts will not awaken it. They merely strengthen opinion; and there is nothing so apt to shut us off from the world as the correct opinion about it. The imagination can be awakened only by the imagination, by the artist who has the power to break us down until the point of secret complicity is reached. It was this point which the writer of romance, undeterred by the day's events, and lost in his world of dramatic wishes, once knew how to reach.

Mr William Golding is an artist of this kind. His three books, *Lord of the Flies* (1954), *The Inheritors* (1955) and *Pincher Martin* (1956), are romance in the austere sense of the term. They take the leap from the probable to the possible. *Lord of the Flies* has a strong pedigree: island literature from Crusoe to *Coral Island*, *Orphan Island* and *High Wind in Jamaica*. All romance breaks with the realistic novelist's certainties and exposes the characters to transcendent and testing dangers. But Golding does more than break; he bashes, by the power of his overwhelming sense of the detail of the physical world. He is the most original of our contemporaries. Many writers have been concerned, as a matter of argument, with what is rhetorically called 'the dilemma of modern man', and have given us, as it were, lantern slide lectures on the anarchy of a poisoned future; they are really essayists sitting in comfort. Golding, on the contrary, scarcely uses an argument or issues a warning. He simply shakes us until we feel in our bones the perennial agony of our species. By their nature, his subjects – prep school boys on a desert island in a world war, the calvary of a sailor who gave the right order but whose half-conscious body is being washed about the gullies of an Atlantic rock, the conflicts of a handful of Neanderthalers – could easily become the pasteboard jigsaw of allegory, pleasing our taste for satire and ingenuity; but the pressure of feeling drives allegory out of the foreground of his stories. He is a writer of intense visual gift, with an overpowering sense of nature and an extraordinary perception of man as a physical being in a physical world, torn between a primitive inheritance and the glimmer of an evolving mind. A dramatic writer and familiar with the strong emotions that go with the instinct of self-preservation – blind love for his kind, hatred, fear and elation – he is without hysteria. He is not cooking up freakish and exotic incident; he is not making large proclamations about man against nature, God, destiny and so on; he is seriously and in precise, individual instances gripped – as if against his will – by the sight of the slow and agonising accretion of a mind and a civilised will in one or two men, struggling against their tendency to slip back, through passion or folly, and lose their skills in panic. And there is pity for the pain they feel.

Pain is the essence of Mr Golding's subject. In *The Inheritors* it is the obscure pain of a baffled and dying group of ape men who see themselves supplanted by the more skilful new being called Man. The ape man experiences the pain of the grunt, of trying to communicate from one poor mind to another – 'I have a picture. Can you see my picture?' – and also the pain of trying to distinguish, for a moment, what is inside from what is outside himself. From his tree he sees Man who is not afraid of water, as he is, who gets drunk on honey, who has invented love play; he sees with a kind of grieving as an animal might grieve. In *Pincher Martin*, the tale of a modern sailor whose broken body is washed about the Atlantic rock, who eats limpets, is poisoned by his store of food and who eventually goes mad and dies, the pain is in the fight against physical hurt and loss of consciousness, in the struggle to put his educated will against his terrors. It is also in the Job-like protest against a defeat which wrongs everything he had believed in. In *Lord of the Flies* – the first and, I think, the best of these books – a group of schoolboys reenact the *Coral Island* story and the pain is in the struggle between the boys who revert, through fear, to the primitive and turn into savage hunters, and those who are trying vainly to preserve foresight and order. In the end, the boys are rescued, but not before they have lived through the modern political nightmare.

Mr Golding's sensibility to pain is the spring of his imagination and if, in all three stories, the heroes are smashed up, he is by no means a morbid or sadistic writer. The chest of the creature, running in terror from its enemies, scorches, the calves cramp, the skin tears, the body has to endure what animal panic lets it in for. Pain is simply the whole condition of man; it is the sign that he is awake and struggling with his nature, and especially with the terror which so suddenly scatters the mind. *Lord of the Flies* contains one episode of great horror. The rotting body of a dead parachutist is blown across the island in the night, almost stepping on the trees and the beaches, until it is taken out to sea. The sight is the final and clinching argument to the very young boys that a devouring Beast has really been among them; and one might conclude that this is a decisive symbol of human defeat and the meaninglessness of the struggle. The idea is irrelevant. Mr Golding's imagination is heroic. Against the flies that buzz round the dangling scarecrow must be put the elation of the adventure, the love of natural life, the curiosity of the eye, that run through the writing. And the compassion.

It is natural to compare *Lord of the Flies* with *Coral Island* – and then with *High Wind in Jamaica*. In *Coral Island* we see the safe community. A century without war and with a settled sense of the human personality has produced it. In Richard Hughes's book, we saw the first sign of disintegration: the psychologists have discovered that children are not small fanciful adults, but are a cut-off, savage race. In *Lord of the Flies* we understand that the children are not cut-off; anthropology, the science of how people live together, not separately, reflects the concern of the modern world which has seen its communities destroyed. The children in *Lord of the Flies* simply re-enact the adult, communal drama and by their easy access to the primitive, show how adult communities can break up. Of course, Mr Golding's improbable romances remain improbable; they are narrow and possible. The modern romancer has the uncluttered chance of going straight to the alienation of the individual and to the personal solitude that is one of the forgotten subjects. In our world, which is so closely organised, we are hardly aware of what we are privately up to. We use large words like calamity, disaster, racial suicide, devastation; they are meaningless to us until an artist appears who is gifted enough to identify himself with a precise body being washed up against a precise collection of rocks, a precise being sniffing the night air for his enemy or feeling the full force of a particular blow. Until then, we are muffled in our alibi: 'the imagination cannot grasp.'

Lord of the Flies is the most accomplished of Mr Golding's novels. Its portraits of the shipwrecked boys and its understanding of them are touching and delightful and he is master of a rich range of scene and action. In this book his spirit and his serenity are classical. *Pincher Martin* is more chock-a-block, but it has fine descriptions of the roaring, sucking, deafening sea scene on the rock which we know stone by stone. He is a modern writer here in that his eyes are pressed close to the object, so that each thing is enormously magnified. We see how much a man is enclosed by his own eyes. The important quality of all Golding's descriptions is that they are descriptions of movement and continuous change and are marked by brilliant epithets. (One remembers: 'three prudish anemones'.) There is this picture of the swimming sailor, almost at the rock: . . . [quotes a passage from the end of the first section of *Pincher Martin*: 'Ropes held him . . . nuzzle under his arm'.]

But this book succeeds less when it takes us into the sailor's

chaotic recollections of his life. It contains some flashes back to
scenes of jealousy and rivalry which are hard to grasp. It may
be that Golding's sense of theatre – often strong in writers of
romance – has overcome him here. (He is the author of a witty
satirical play, *The Brass Butterfly*, which is excellent reading.)
But in making us feel in the current of the modern world,
instead of being stranded and deadened by it; in providing us
with secret parables; in unveiling important parts of the
contemporary anguish and making them heroic, knowable and
imaginable, he is unique.

SOURCE: essay in *New Statesman* (2 Aug. 1958), pp. 146–7.

Frank Kermode   'Golding's Intellectual Economy'   (1962)

The critical reception of Mr Golding's fourth novel, *Free Fall*
(1959), was on the whole hostile; that of its predecessor (*Pincher
Martin*, 1956) uncomprehending. Not since his first, *Lord of the
Flies* (1954), has he enjoyed general acclaim; yet the opinion
that he is the most important practising novelist in England
has, over this period of five or six years, become almost
commonplace. One reason for this apparent paradox is that
Golding's books do not (if only because each is extremely
original in construction) yield themselves at one reading: *The
Inheritors* (1955) and *Pincher Martin* have been better understood
with the passing of time, and the same will be true of *Free Fall*.
This suggests that Golding is a difficult writer; and it would not
be strange if this were true. We have become accustomed, for
intelligible historical reasons, to the idea that significant works
of art are necessarily obscure.

It is, however, true only in a limited sense. We may note at
once that despite the roar of baffled critics Mr Golding's
intentions are always simple. Of *Pincher Martin* he says 'I fell

over backwards in making that novel explicit. I said to myself, "Now here is going to be a novel, it's going to be a blow on behalf of the ordinary universe, which I think on the whole likely to be the right one, and I'm going to write it so vividly and accurately and with such an exact programme that nobody can possibly mistake exactly what I mean." '[1] But he goes on to admit that his handling of the story was 'unspecific'; he did not actually *tell* the reader that Martin drowns on page 2; the evidence that he did so is oblique, and is completed only by the last sentence of the book. Golding is unlike many modern writers in his willingness to state the 'programme' of his book (and also in denying the reader much liberty of interpretation); but he does not pretend that what seems to him simple must be so explicitly and directly set down that the reader will not have to work. In short, his simplicity is a quality best understood as intellectual economy. His theme takes the simplest available way to full embodiment. But embodiment is not explanation; and all that can be guaranteed the reader is that there is no *unnecessary* difficulty, nothing to make the business of explaining and understanding more difficult than, in the nature of the case, it has to be.

The best course for sympathetic critics is to be a shade more explicit, to do what the novelist himself perhaps cannot do without injury to the books, which grow according to imaginative laws, and cannot be adjusted to the extravagant needs of readers. If critics have any reason for existence, this is it; to give assurances of value, and to provide somehow – perhaps anyhow – the means by which readers may be put in possession of the valuable book.

It is worth notice that Golding is to a marked degree isolated from intellectual fashion: 'I think that my novels have very little genesis outside myself. That to a large extent I've cut myself off from contemporary literary life, and gained in one sense by it, though I may have lost in another.' He is more interested in Greek than in modern literature. Thus there are in his books preoccupations one would not expect in a highbrow modern novelist – that Ballantyne was wrong about the behaviour of English boys on a desert island, or H. G. Wells about the virtue of Neanderthal men, are not opinions many would care to dispute, but few would find in them points of departure for passionate and involved fictions. In the same way Mr Golding, though he is in some degree an allegorical writer, is entirely free of Kafka's influence, which makes him very unlike Rex Warner, with whom he is sometimes implausibly compared. His technical equipment is as sophisticated as Conrad's; yet like Conrad he begins each new book as if it were his first, as if the germination of the new theme entailed the creation of its own incomparable form. (There are, however, some habitual devices – the sudden shift of viewpoint at the end of the first three novels, for instance.) Perhaps the resemblance to Conrad could be developed: an isolated indeed exiled sensibility, a preoccupation with guilt, desperate technical resource. Sometimes this last power re-invests what others have done before, old devices labelled in text-books: stream of consciousness, changing point of view, time-shifts. There was a time according to the author himself, when he wrote novels intended to meet the requirements of the public, as far as he could guess them; but these novels failed, were never even published. Then, with *Lord of the Flies*, he saw that it was himself he had to satisfy; he planned it in very great detail, and wrote it as if tracing over words already on the page. How, in pleasing his own isolated taste, and doing it in these essentially unmodish and rather private ways, has he come to represent to so many the best in modern English writing?

The answer to this is necessarily involved, though the situation is in itself simple enough. One thinks of Mr Golding's world: he sees it swinging through its space, its wet or rocky surfaces lifting under the pull of the moon; its inhabitants, locked on to it by gravity, walking upright, containing floating brains, peristaltic entrails, secreting seed at the base of the spine, somehow free and somehow guilty. Golding once called himself 'a propagandist for Neanderthal man'; his way of looking at the world has something of the candour of Lascaux. In *The Inheritors* Neanderthal man is superseded by *homo sapiens*, who has a better brain, and weapons; but it is the innocence of the doomed predecessor that we see enacted, for, until the last pages, we see the activities of the new man, intelligent and so capable of evil, through the bewildered eyes of the old. And

Golding, though he admits that we belong with the new man, supposes that we could not recapture that innocence, that natural awe for Oa, the mother-goddess, had not something of it survived in us.

I am groping for an answer to the question, how such a writer can strike us as profoundly attuned to contemporary sensibility? It seems to be that in his own way, and short-circuiting a great deal of fashionable and sophisticated mythologising, Golding gives remarkably full expression to a profound modern need, the need for reassurance in terms of the primitive; the longing to know somehow of a possible humanity that lived equably in the whole world; the need for myths of total and satisfactory explanation. Our developed consciousness, our accumulated knowledge are marks of guilt; the fragmentary nature of our experience is the theme of our artists. To discover again the undifferentiated myth is to return to Eden or to Neanderthal man – or indeed to the primary germ-cell the splitting of which is the beginning of guilt: that is to find innocence and wisdom.

Golding has been called a writer of 'fables'; 'what I would regard as a tremendous compliment to myself', he says, 'would be if someone would substitute the word "myth" for "fable". . . . I do feel fable as being an invented thing on the surface whereas myth is something which comes out from the roots of things in the ancient sense of being the key to existence, the whole meaning of life, and experience as a whole.' And he accepts the description, 'myths of total explanation', for his works. The genesis of these myths is naturally obscure. They do not much resemble the myths of Joyce or those of Mr Eliot or Mr David Jones; yet they are related to the same Symbolist aspirations towards prelogical primitive images which animate all these authors. The differences are attributable to Mr Golding's relative isolation from any mainstream of speculation. To put it too simply: he sees a world enormously altered by new knowledge. He understands the strong reaction against this new knowledge which is characteristic of modern art, an art in love with the primitive; also the patterns of human behaviour are now very generally explained by reference to psychic residua or infantile guilt. It is a world you can blame 'science' for if you like, a world in which the myth of progress has failed; but the rival myth of necessary evil and universal guilt has come back without bringing God with it. He looks at this world understanding what it contains, as the painters at Lascaux understood theirs. He thinks of the books of his childhood – *Coral Island*, Wells' *Outline of History* – and observes that they are wrong about the world, because they thought cannibals more wicked than white men and Neanderthal man less worthy than his conqueror. These books have, in his own figure, rotted to compost in his mind; and in that compost the new myth puts down roots. When it grows it explains the ancient situation to which our anxieties recall us: loss of innocence, the guilt and ignominy of consciousness, the need for pardon. Mr Golding owns that he is a religious man. He believes that some people are saints: in *Lord of the Flies* Simon is a saint, and this is why, he says, literary people have found Simon incomprehensible; 'but he *is* comprehensible to the illiterate person. . . . The illiterate person believes in saints and sanctity.' (This is not the first time a modern artist has found his allies among the illiterate – Yeats and Eliot have made similar declarations.) Golding believes in human guilt and the human sense of paradise lost; he also believes in divine mercy.

The evidence for holiness lies scattered among the fragments of our world, and those fragments are represented in Golding's books; they form part of the whole. But this whole is a world of imagination, where everything is related, everything counts and truth is accessible: the world of myth. For Golding's own term is the right one; out of the single small seed grows this instrument 'for controlling . . . ordering . . . giving a shape and significance to the immense paradox of futility and anarchy which is contemporary history'. These are Mr Eliot's words on Joyce's myth; but they will serve for Golding. Art, says Cassirer, requires a step back into mythical thinking; perhaps this has always been so since mythical thinking became obsolete, but never has the step back been more consciously taken than in our times. And in the contrast between our consciousness of this, and the momentary forgetfulness of our Darwinian grandfathers, Golding found the theme of his first novel.

Lord of the Flies has 'a pretty big connection' with Ballantyne. In *The Coral Island* Ralph, Jack and Peterkin are cast away on a desert island, where they live active, civilised, and civilising lives. Practical difficulties are easily surmounted; they light fires with bowstrings and spyglasses, hunt pigs for food, and kill them with much ease and a total absence of guilt – indeed of bloodshed. They are all Britons – a term they use to compliment each other – all brave, obedient and honourable. There is much useful information conveyed concerning tropical islands, including field-workers' reporting of the conduct of cannibals: but anthropology is something nasty that clears up on the arrival of a missionary, and Jack himself prevents an act of cannibalism by telling the flatnoses not to be such blockheads and presenting them with six newly slaughtered pigs. The parallel between the island and the Earthly Paradise causes a trace of literary sophistication: 'Meat and drink on the same tree! My dear boys, we're set up for life; it must be the ancient paradise – hurrah! . . . We afterwards found, however, that these lovely islands were very unlike Paradise in many things.' But these 'things' are non-Christian natives and, later, pirates; the boys themselves are cleanly (cold baths recommended) and godly – regenerate, empire-building boys, who know by instinct how to turn paradise into a British protectorate.

The Coral Island (1858) could be used as a document in the history of ideas; it belongs inseparably to the period when boys were sent out of Arnoldian schools certified free of Original Sin. Golding takes Ralph, Jack and Peterkin (altering this name to Simon, 'called Peter') and studies them against an altered moral landscape. He is a schoolmaster, and knows boys well enough to make their collapse into savagery plausible, to see *them* as the cannibals; the authority of the grown-ups is all there is to prevent savagery. If you dropped these boys into an Earthly Paradise 'they would not behave like God-fearing English gentlemen' but 'as like as not . . . find savages who were kindly and uncomplicated. . . . The devil would rise out of the intellectual complications of the three white men.' Golding leaves the noble savages out of *Lord of the Flies* but this remark is worth quoting because it states the intellectual position in its basic simplicity. It is the civilised who are corrupt, out of phase

with natural rhythm. Their guilt is the price of evolutionary
success; and our awareness of this fact can be understood by
duplicating Ballantyne's situation, borrowing his island, and
letting his theme develop in this new and more substantial
context. Once more every prospect pleases; but the vileness
proceeds, not from cannibals, but from the boys, though Man is
not so much vile as 'heroic and sick'. Unlike Ballantyne's boys,
these are dirty and inefficient; they have some notion of order,
symbolised by the beautiful conch which heralds formal
meetings; but when uncongenial effort is required to maintain
it, order disappears. The shelters are inadequate, the signal fire
goes out at the very moment when Jack first succeeds in killing
a pig. Intelligence fades; irrational taboos and blood-rituals
make hopeless the task of the practical but partial intellect of
Piggy; his glasses, the firemakers, are smashed and stolen, and
in the end he himself is broken to pieces as he holds the conch.
When civilised conditioning fades – how tedious Piggy's appeal
to what adults might do or think! – the children are capable of
neither savage nor civil gentleness. Always a little nearer to raw
humanity than adults, they slip into a condition of animality
depraved by mind, into the cruelty of hunters with their
devil-liturgies and torture. They make an unnecessary, evil
fortress, they steal, they abandon all operations aimed at
restoring them to civility. Evil is the natural product of their
consciousness. First the smallest boys create a beastie, a snake –
'as if it wasn't a good island'. Then a beast is created in good
earnest, and defined in a wonderful narrative sequence. The
emblem of this evil society is the head of a dead pig, fixed, as a
sacrifice, on the end of a stick and animated by flies and by the
imagination of the *voyant*, Simon.

   Simon is Golding's first 'saint, and a most important figure'.
He is 'for the illiterate a proof of the existence of God' because
the illiterate (to whom we are tacitly but unmistakably
expected to attribute a correct insight here) will say, 'Well, a
person like this cannot exist without a good God'. For Simon
'voluntarily embraces the beast . . . and tries to get rid of him'.
What he understands – and this is wisdom Golding treats with
awe – is that evil is 'only us'. He climbs up to where the dead fire
is dominated by the beast, a dead airman in a parachute,

discovers what this terrible thing really is, and rushes off with the good news to the beach, where the maddened boys at their beast-slaying ritual mistake Simon himself for the beast and kill him. As Piggy, the dull practical intelligence, is reduced to blindness and futility, so Simon, the visionary, is murdered before he can communicate his comfortable knowledge. Finally, the whole Paradise is destroyed under the puzzled eyes of an adult observer. Boys will be boys.

The difference of this world from Ballantyne's simpler construction from similar materials is not merely a matter of incomparability of the two talents at work; our minds have, in general, darker needs and obscurer comforts. It would be absurd to suppose that the change has impoverished us; but it has seemed to divide our world into 'two cultures' – the followers of Jack and the admirers of Simon, those who build fortresses and those who want to name the beast.

Lord of the Flies was 'worked out carefully in every possible way', and its author holds that the 'programme' of the book *is* its meaning. He rejects Lawrence's doctrine, 'Never trust the artist, trust the tale' and its consequence, 'the proper function of the critic is to save the tale from the artist'. He is wrong, I think; in so far as the book differs from its programme there is, as a matter of common sense, material over which the writer has no absolute authority. This means not only that there are possible readings which he cannot veto, but even that some of his own views on the book may be in a sense wrong. The interpretation of the dead parachutist is an example. This began in the 'programme' as straight allegory; Golding says that this dead man 'is' History. 'All that we can give our children' in their trouble is this monstrous dead adult, who's 'dead, but won't lie down'; an ugly emblem of war and decay that broods over the paradise and provides the only objective equivalent for the beast the boys imagine. Now this limited allegory (I may even have expanded it in the telling) seems to me not to have got out of the 'programme' into the book; what does get in is more valuable because more like myth – capable, that is, of more various interpretation than the rigidity of Golding's scheme allows. And in writing of this kind all depends upon the author's mythopoeic power to transcend the 'programme'. Golding has this poetic power, and nowhere is it more impressively used than in his second book, *The Inheritors*.

Prefixed to *The Inheritors* is a passage from Wells's *Outline of History*, and this serves the same purpose as Ballantyne's novel in the genesis of the earlier book; it sets off an antithetical argument. 'Wells's *Outline* played a great part in my life because my father was a rationalist, and the *Outline* was something he took neat. It is the rationalist gospel *in excelsis*. . . . By and by it seemed to me not to be large enough . . . too neat and too slick. And when I re-read it as an adult I came across his picture of Neanderthal man, our immediate predecessors, as being these gross, brutal creatures who were possibly the basis of the mythological bad man . . . I thought to myself that this is just absurd. . . .' The difference between Golding and the Wells of the *Outline* is simple; to Wells the success of the high-foreheaded, weapon-bearing, carnivorous *homo sapiens* was progress, but to Golding it was the defeat of innocence, the sin of Adam in terms of a new kind of history.

Golding's real power, the true nature of his mythopoeic obsession, became evident only with the publication of this second book. This root-idea is, as I have suggested, a variant of the Fall, transplanted from theology. Golding is fascinated by the evidence – in the nature of the case ubiquitous – that human consciousness is a biological asset purchased at a price; the price is the knowledge of evil. This evil emanates from the human mind, a product of its action upon the environment. *The Inheritors* is about the accumulation of guilt that necessarily attended the historical success of *homo sapiens*; the intellectual superiority of Man over his simian victims is precisely measured by the cruelty and guilt which dominate his life and are relatively absent from his predecessor's. The creatures to be exterminated are almost innocent, as near it as we can imagine; they practise no deceit, have an obscure sense of life as a mystery, understand wickedness as killing, but their lives are controlled by the seasons, by inhibiting fears of water, above all by a physiological equipment excellent in its way but prohibiting intellect. They know the world with senses like an animal's; they depend much upon involuntary reflexes – keen scent, night vision, acuteness of ear; they are not men at all, and that is why they are innocent. Only after prolonged observations of the new men can Lok associate sex with cruelty, derange his senses with alcohol, offer violence to a friend, or even think of one thing or process as 'like' another. Not to know evil is, in a sense, to know nothing. The new men sail away, successful and guilty, leaving Lok with the doll-goddess which is his only image of the intelligent and creative mind. Clutching this toy, he who had known useful fear is now the prey of useless terror as well as of his animal enemies; they, the real creators, plan a bloody and intelligent future.

Technically *The Inheritors* attempts a little less than *Pincher Martin*, but has fewer flaws. The natural setting, of obvious importance, needed to be wonderfully done and is. Above all, the feat of recording observations of the activities of *homo sapiens* made with the sensory equipment of Lok is of astonishing virtuosity. We are constantly reminded of the involuntary powers that sustain him; his ears speak to him even if he will not listen, small areas of skin react with useful knowledge, the nose marvellously distinguishes and identifies. We can always see, too, that the extinction of this animal is *necessary*, as in the passage where he observes a new man aiming at him with a bow and can no more conceive of what the man is doing than he can impute enmity to so similar a being or explain his tall face – his senses simply report a series of inexplicable events. In the heart of the book there is a remarkable passage of some fifty pages in which Lok and the female Fa observe the communal activities of the new people from a vantage-point in a tree. This is carried out with a fierce imaginative power that is not in the least inconsistent with a very minute attention to the complicated effect to be communicated. What we have to be shown is that, although we are experiencing these events innocently, by way of the passive, vegetarian, inhuman senses of Lok, we *belong* down below in the clearing, corrupt and intelligent. And at the end we abruptly leave Lok; suddenly, with a loss of sympathy, observe him with our normal sight, joining the new men, our own sort. With these anxious and responsible technicians we sail away, with only a last glimpse of superseded innocence stumbling about on the shore of a dead world. *The Inheritors* does not, like *Lord of the Flies*, qualify as a spanking good tale, and with its publication Golding met for the first time that uncomprehending reception with which he is now so familiar. The book was written, presumably at white-heat, in a few weeks. It has not been surpassed.

Pincher Martin is, however, a bigger book. It is another imaginative 'forcing' of the same seminal idea, but more densely written, with much interweaving of image and reference – more like a poem, in fact, for undoubtedly this kind of novel 'aspires' to the condition of poetry. It takes more reading than the others; it lacks the adventitious accessibility of *Lord of the Flies* and is less recognisably a story than *The Inheritors*. For all that, its wisp of narrative is handled with great skill, and after all the full import of the book depends upon a most ingenious narrative device. The talent remains clearly that which produced the earlier books, and some of the procedures, particularly those involving the extraction of significance from symbolic objects, are easy to recognise. And there is a continuity of theme. But it is, all the same, a book demanding unremitting attention.

Golding has himself provided 'a mental lifeline' to readers who find the book difficult; it appeared in *Radio Times* and it might be useful to copy part of what he said.

Christopher Hadley Martin had no belief in anything but the importance of his own life, no God. Because he was created in the image of God he had a freedom of choice which he used to centre the world on himself. He did not believe in purgatory and therefore when he died it was not presented to him in overtly theological terms. The greed for life which had been the mainspring of his nature forced him to refuse the selfless act of dying. He continued to exist separately in a world composed of his own murderous nature. His drowned body lies rolling in the Atlantic but the ravenous ego invents a rock for him to endure on. It is the memory of an aching tooth. Ostensibly and rationally he is a survivor from a torpedoed destroyer: but deep down he knows the truth. He is not fighting for bodily survival but for his continuing identity in face of what will smash it and sweep it away – the black lightning, the compassion of God. For Christopher, the Christ-bearer, has become Pincher Martin who is little but greed. Just to be Pincher is purgatory; to be Pincher for eternity is hell.

The man is called Martin so that his worldly name may be Pincher (a naval nickname for all Martins) and nobody calls him 'Christopher' until God does so at the end, out of the black lightning, as the resisting Martin shrinks to a mere pair of claws. Again the myth is worked out in fanatical detail; Martin calls his rock 'Rockall' not only because that is a real rock, but because he remembers a poor joke turning on a word which is a bad rhyme for Rockall, and which is an obscene word for 'nothing'. The geology and animal life of the rock he invents out of memories of childhood holidays. He is horribly aware of the self-deceit, the Promethean posing, the shrinking identity; he will do anything rather than accept the loss of himself, even in exchange for the mercy of God.

Martin is 'fallen man – fallen more than most'; a type of depravity. His human consciousness is an evolutionary specialisation, like a pig's snout, used to ensure handsome survival. He is hideously greedy, hence the recurrent metaphors from eating. 'He takes the best part [Martin had been an actor], the best seat, the most money, the best notice, the best woman. He was born with his mouth and his flies open and both hands out to grab. He's a cosmic case of the bugger who gets his penny and someone else's bun.' But this efficiency only makes his suffering more characteristic; he declares for madness rather than extinction, intellect rather than love, and makes his own most appropriate purgatory. Martin's boast is that he controls and imposes his will on the world: 'I can outwit you; you are a machine.' He is relieved to discover that the cause of apparently 'evil' manifestations lie entirely within himself; that his fear of the gull which makes him think of lizards originates in something he's read; that he can cure the world by curing his own disorder. There is a crucial and astonishing episode in which, with all the gestures of heroism, he undertakes to expel the poison from within him. He has eaten disgusting food, and it has made his mind sick as well as his body. 'I am in servitude to a coiled tube the length of a cricket pitch. All the terrors of hell can come down to nothing more than a stoppage. Why drag in good and evil when the serpent lies coiled in my own body?' His intelligent solution is a self-inflicted enema.

But although it is true that the evil proceeds from within him, it will not be dispersed by intelligence. That only preserves him alive for torture, and he creates his hell with the same effort that he puts forth to preserve his identity. Of the plenitude with which this and all the related paradoxes inherent in the theme are developed I have room to say virtually nothing. But one of them requires notice, since I argue for the totality of the imaginative act. Martin's acts are willed, but also necessary; and this is beautifully translated into narrative at the point where, as officer of the watch, he gives a helm-order a moment before the torpedo strikes. The order was freely willed and murderous; it was also necessary and proper in the circumstance. All that happened was 'because of what I did', but it could not have been otherwise. Only the best in fiction has invention of this order.

This is not quite the whole story. It would seem, as a hypothesis stemming from the situation described, that another heaven might be possible, a God to whom some other question than 'If I ate them, who gave me a mouth?' might be addressed. Golding's Nathaniel, whose natural goodness Martin recognises and resents, is there to say that only in the abandonment of the beloved self is there any way to this. Nathaniel is the second in what may be a band of Golding's elect, those who see and know. But Nathaniel is anything but a respectable saint; his religion has a seedy quality and it contributes to Martin's agony as well as shadowing it with some ecstatic alternative. It isn't a pill of doctrine but another part of the imaginative structure.

Pincher Martin is a wonderful achievement, the book of a drowned man soaked and battered by an actual sea, making substantial rock out of nightmare; it is as if one's own hands grew soft and swollen in the idiot water and bruised on the dripping stone. It is a horrible book too; because the man is shrunk so mercilessly into his minimal disgusting humanity, the fattest maggot of all; and because Golding's knowledge of human egotism and cruelty is horrible. What makes all this bearable and Golding a major novelist is the total technical control: nightmare, hysteria, every kind of beastliness and depravity are given the virtue of form. There is no distinguishing here between a compassion that might be called religious and the skill of an artist; they are the same thing.

There are those who find Golding sadistic; it is a judgement that calls in question their ability to read any book whatsoever, because it betrays an insensitivity to the moral quality of form. Yeats spoke of an intellectual construct which enabled him to 'hold in a single thought reality and justice'; *Pincher Martin* is such a thought.

Of *Free Fall*, Golding's fourth and perhaps his most ambitious book, I must say that although I do not feel that I have yet got to know it well I have no expectation that it can ever possess my mind as the others have done. It should be remembered that Golding asks a lot of his critics – this is a matter, I think, of emphasis, of his not saying 'The first page and the last page are crucial'. He does not say so because it seems to him self-evident.[2] It is not in such reticences that Mr Golding fails (if he does fail); for in everything related to the shape of this myth his skill is all that it was in *Pincher Martin*. Technically *Free Fall* (which depends upon a system of 'time-shifts' devised to expose the religious significance of a man's experience) is at least as accomplished as any of the others. It is a mark of Golding's integrity that in every book he employs technical devices of remarkable ingenuity but never indulges his skill; it is never a hair's-breadth in excess of what the moral occasion demands. One's coolness towards the book has other causes.

The myth of *Free Fall* is, basically, that of all Golding's books: the Fall of Man, the expulsion from Paradise, erected wit and infected will. It is a myth which has accumulated an enormous and various theology, which does not matter until the novelist turns theologian himself. Golding's hero is examining his life (made typical life by many allegorical devices) with a view to discovering a pattern, some connection between his two worlds of experience, one deterministic, the world of empirical observation, the other a world in which the burning bush is not consumed, a world of horror and glory, heaven and hell. Sammy's conclusion (which is not the conclusion of the novel) is that 'there is no bridge'. In his brooding over different episodes in his life, Sammy Mountjoy is necessarily theologising; in other words, there is within the book continuous comment – admittedly not directly vouched for by the author –

on the myth. I do not think that this works; there is an unwonted hollowness in these passages, the shabbiness of a do-it-yourself theology; and the book at moments lies open to the Coleridgean charge of mental bombast – 'thoughts and images too great for the subject' – the subject being not the Fall but a *commentary* upon it. In Golding's earlier books – and this is unique in modern fiction – guilt, unconscious innocence, the taste of isolation, good and evil, are made actual, like vomit in the mouth. It is this actuality that is lacking in *Free Fall*; its absence takes the nature out of Golding's prose, it takes the plasticity out of the narrative. The crucial episode, a nightmare experience in a prison-cell, calls for, and is not provided with, the savage compassion which went into the writing of *Pincher Martin*. Yet it is in a way wonderfully composed, passionate and cunning; there is no question of a failure of power or of nerve, only – to be bold – of a flaw in the original conception.

This flaw is one to which Mr Golding's gifts render him peculiarly liable. Myths of total explanation are religious; comment upon them is theology. *Free Fall*, like *Paradise Lost*, is about *everything*; the author knows this, devises his narrative and even names his characters accordingly. Samuel Mountjoy at first misunderstands his vocation (like Samuel in the Bible) and is as a child in his slum an inhabitant of Paradise (Mountjoy). As he writes, he lives on Paradise Hill, 'thirty seconds from the shop and the local'. A central event of his life is the recognition of the beauty of a girl called Beatrice; later, by a positive act of will, he rejects the possibility of living by this vision, and subjects her to his lust. The two worlds between which his life is suspended (in a condition of 'free fall' as understood in science fiction) are represented by a religious schoolmistress and a science master called Nick. The child does not have to choose; in childhood the two worlds interlock. He chooses, as a young man, to desecrate Beatrice. The other world he finds again in a prison-camp, where he is subjected by a German officer named Halde[3] to an interrogation modelled on that of Christ in the desert. Will he reject the 'world'? Is he a son of God? He does not know enough to betray his comrades, and Halde sends him to a cell which he peoples with his own egotistical terrors; at the height of his agony he bursts out (or is let out) of the cell, forgiven. He walks into the world of vision: 'The power of gravity, dimension and space, the movement of the earth and sun and unseen stars, these made what might be called music and I heard it.' Beatrice has been reduced (and this passage is as fine as anything in Golding) to an incontinent idiot in an asylum; but Sammy still finds himself called to Paradise. He cannot reconcile the two worlds but the novelist, on the last page, builds a kind of bridge between them.

That it is mythologically substantial, this bridge, I do not doubt; but I do not understand it. The novel is about delivery from the body of this death; not only about the Fall but also about regeneration. This account of it is too scanty to be fair even to my imperfect understanding of the book, but it may be enough to help me make my point: that it is not the religious but the theological element that limits the imaginative scope, and brings into the writing a kind of dry heat, a brittleness, absent before. I ought to say that Messrs Gregor and Kinkead-Weekes, in the intelligent article I have already quoted [viz., end-note 2 – Ed.] find the theology satisfactory, and indeed orthodox. But Mr Golding is not orthodox. He has done what writers in the Romantic tradition have done before – as Mallarmé discovered Nirvana without knowing Buddhism, or as Yeats dwelt, though heretically, on the Annunciation, he has found in experience and embodied in his own myths the truths that inform all others. But to provide accounts of mystical experience is one thing – admittedly a difficult thing, if only because of the qualitative differences between St John of the Cross and a mescalin addict; to invent a mystical theology is another. The first is work for a genius, the second for a church. Not to see this is the flaw of all the Romantic and Symbolist writers who lapsed into the pseudo-theologies of occultism.

A final word on 'simplicity'. Golding's novels are simple in so far as they deal in the primordial patterns of human experience and in so far as they have skeletons of parable. On these simple bones the flesh of narrative can take extremely complex forms. This makes for difficulty, but of the most acceptable kind, the difficulty that attends the expression of what is profoundly simple. For all that I have said against *Free Fall* it is this kind of book, like the others a work of genius by a writer from whom we can hope for much more, since he is in superbly full possession of his great powers.

SOURCE: essay 'William Golding' (incorporating material written 1958–60, including parts of Professor Kermode's BBC interview with the novelist in 1959), in *Puzzles and Epiphanies* (London, 1962), pp. 198–213.

NOTES

[Renumbered from the original – Ed.]

1. This, and several other remarks attributed to Mr Golding in this article, are derived from a transcript of a BBC discussion programme. [Professor Kermode's interview with Golding was broadcast on the BBC Third Programme (28 Aug. 1959) and published in *Books and Bookmen*, V (Oct. 1959), pp. 9–10 – Ed.]

2. There is a perceptive study of the opening and the conclusion of *Free Fall* in an article by Ian Gregor and M. Kinkead-Weekes called 'Mr Golding and his Critics' in *Twentieth Century* (Feb. 1960).

3. It has been pointed out that *Halde* means 'slope', and that this name is also allegorical, since Halde is the agent by which Sammy moves into the gravitational field of his spiritual work. Mr Golding tells me he did not think of this. It is allegorist's luck.

James Gindin   'Gimmick' and Metaphor in the Novels of William Golding   (1960)

William Golding has written four novels: *Lord of the Flies* (1954); *The Inheritors* (1955); *Pincher Martin* (1956); *Free Fall* (1959). Each of the first three novels demonstrates the use of unusual and striking literary devices. Each is governed by a massive metaphorical structure – a man clinging for survival to a rock in the Atlantic Ocean or an excursion into the mind of man's evolutional antecedent – designed to assert something permanent and significant about human nature. The metaphors are intensive, far-reaching, permeate all the details and events of the novels. Yet, at the end of each of the novels, the metaphors, unique and striking as they are, turn into 'gimmicks', into clever tricks that shift the focus or the emphasis of the novel as a whole. And, in each case, the 'gimmick seems to work against the novel, to contradict or to limit the range of reference and meaning that Golding has already established metaphorically. The turn from metaphor to 'gimmick' (and 'gimmick' is the word that Golding himself has applied to his own endings) raises questions concerning the unity and, perhaps more important, the meaning of the novels.

Golding's first novel, *Lord of the Flies*, tells the story of a group of English schoolboys, between the ages of six and twelve, who survive a plane crash on a tropical island. The boys were apparently evacuated during a destructive atomic war and are left, with no adult control anywhere about, to build their own society on the island. The chance to create a new Paradise is clear enough, but Golding quickly indicates that the boys are products of and intrinsically parts of current human society. Even on the very first page: 'The fair boy stopped and jerked his stockings with an automatic gesture that made the jungle seem for a moment like the Home Counties.' The island provides food, plenty of opportunity for swimming, and 'fun'. But a conflict quickly develops between the boys, led by Ralph, who would keep a fire going (they cherish some hope of rescue) and build adequate shelters and those, led by Jack, originally members of a choir, who would hunt wild pigs and give full reign to their predatory and savage instincts. In the first, democratic, meeting, Ralph wins most of the boys' votes, is elected the leader of the island. But the rational democracy is not able to cope very well with the fears of the younger boys, the occasional tendency to rash mob action, the terror of the unexplained 'beast' that fills the night. Gradually, Jack gains more followers. He paints himself in savage colors, neglects to tend the fire because he is mercilessly tracking down a wild pig, establishes a wild and ritualistic dance that fascinates the boys. When one of the boys, having discovered the rational truth of the 'beast' at the top of the mountain (the 'beast' is a dead man in his parachute, dropped from a battle ten miles above the island), stumbles into the ritualistic dance, he is forced by Jack to enact the role of the pig. The boy is never given the time or the opportunity to make the rational truth clear, for the dancers, cloaked in frenzy and darkness, kill him. Ralph is unable to stop the others, even, to his shame, recognises some of the same dark frenzy at the center of his own being. And Piggy, Ralph's 'brain trust' though always unattractive and unpopular, the boy whose glasses got the fire going in the first place, is killed by Jack's principal lieutenant. Jack is victorious. His dogmatic authority, his cruelty and his barbaric frenzy have a deeper hold on the nature of man than do Ralph's sensible regulations. The forces of light and reason fail to alleviate the predatory brutality and the dark, primeval fear at the center of man.

But the metaphor of the society the boys construct is not left to do its work alone. Just when the savage forces led by Jack are tracking down Ralph and burning the whole island to find him, a British naval officer arrives to rescue the boys. Ironically, the smoke of barbaric fury, not the smoke of conscious effort, has led to rescue. Throughout the novel, frequent references to possible rescue and to the sanity of the adult world seemed the delusions of the rational innocent. Ralph and Piggy often appealed to adult sanity in their futile attempt to control their world, but, suddenly and inconsistently at the end of the novel, adult sanity really exists. The horror of the boys' experience on the island was really a childish game, though a particularly vicious one, after all. The British officer turns into a public school master: 'I should have thought that a pack of British boys – you're all British aren't you? – would have been able to put up a better show than that.' The officer's density is apparent, but the range of the whole metaphor has been severely limited. Certainly, the whole issue, the whole statement about man, is not contradicted by the ending, for, as Golding directly points out, Ralph has learned from the experience: 'And in the middle of them, with filthy body, matted hair, and unwiped nose, Ralph wept for the end of innocence, the darkness of man's heart, and the fall through the air of the true, wise friend called Piggy.' But the rescue is ultimately a 'gimmick', a trick, a means of cutting down or softening the implications built up within the structure of the boys' society on the island.

Golding's second novel, *The Inheritors*, relates the story of the last family of man's ancestors, conquered and supplanted by man. The family of 'people' (Golding's word for the heavy, hairy, ape-like forerunners of man) migrate to their spring home and slowly realise that things have changed, slowly discover the encroachments of a tribe of 'others' (men). The 'people' are not capable of thinking, of abstraction and of forming rational connections. They simply act by instinct and 'have pictures', many of which they do not understand. Yet, for all their perceptual and intellectual limitations, the 'people' have a code of ethics (they will not kill other animals, though they do eat the meat of animals already killed), a deep and humble sense of their own limitations, and a faith in the divine power and goodness of the earth. In addition, the 'people' enjoy a family life free from fighting, guilt and emotional squabbling. Each has his function, carefully defined and limited, each his respect for the other members of the family. The novel is the process of man conquering the 'people', capturing or killing them one by one. The last of the 'people' is able to watch man, to understand dimly man's power and victory. But this last survivor of the 'people' is also able to sense in what ways man is a creature different from the 'people'. He watches man brawl and fight, steal other men's mates, suffer guilt and anxiety, tear himself apart between his real ability and his failure to exceed his limitations. The novel carries the implication that man's unique power to reason and think carries with it his propensity toward pride and sin and guilt, toward those qualities that cause him pain and misery.

Most of the novel is told from the point of view of the last of the 'people', a humble creature who depicts the issues without fully understanding them. The last chapter, however, provides a switch in point of view, for it is seen through the eyes of one of the men after the 'people', the 'devils' in human terminology, have been wiped out. The theme does not change: man sees himself as a being tortured by pride and guilt, one who has faith in his power but continually runs into conflict with other men and with his own limitations. Here, the 'gimmick' does not change or vitiate the point of the novel. Rather, the 'gimmick', the switch in point of view, merely repeats what the rest of the novel has already demonstrated. Awareness and rational intelligence are still inextricably connected with human sin, and the 'gimmick' at the end of the novel breaks the unity without adding relevant perspective. The contrast between the 'people' and men is more effectively detailed, made more sharply applicable and relevant, when dimly apprehended by the last of the 'people'.

Man's capacity to reason is again ineffectual in Golding's third novel, *Pincher Martin*. Christopher Martin ('Pincher' because he has presumably stolen almost everything he's ever had), a naval officer, is blown into the North Atlantic when a submarine attacks his ship. Fighting the water and shrieking for rescue, he eventually finds a rock in the middle of the ocean. He laboriously makes his way to the surface of the rock. Convinced of his health, his education and his intelligence, he consciously sets about organising his routine, naming places, gathering food, doing all that rational man can do to insure his survival and rescue, his ultimate salvation. But time and weather, forces stronger than he, in addition to his guilty consciousness of past sins (brought up through his memory of his past as actor, seducer, pincher of whatever his friends had), wear down the rational man. All his rational efforts fail and he is pushed by nature, both external and internal, toward death and damnation.

The conflict between survival and extinction is extended by a consistent use of microcosmic imagery. When Martin first sees the rock, Golding writes: 'A single point of rock, peak of a mountain range, one tooth set in the ancient jaw of a sunken world, projecting through the inconceivable vastness of the whole ocean.' The rock is constantly compared with a tooth of the world; the struggles taking place on the rock are a mirror of the struggles taking place all over the world. Martin's battle for survival is imagistically made the battle of all men for salvation, a battle in which reason, sanity and careful order are not enough. As the rock is imagistically linked to the larger world, so is Martin himself made a kind of universal focus. His head is frequently a 'globe', his own teeth are linked to the shape of the rock: 'His tongue was remembering. It pried into the gap between the teeth and re-created the old, aching shape. It touched the rough edge of the cliff, traced the slope down, trench after aching trench . . . understood what was so hauntingly familiar and painful about an isolated and decaying rock in the middle of the sea.'

Similarly, the issues of Martin's salvation or damnation are presented within his own body. He sometimes feels his 'center' in conflict with the memory of his loins. His eyes are 'windows'. The forces of nature that defeat him are linked to forces within himself. Ocean currents are tongues; the mind is a 'stirred pudding': '. . . how can the stirred pudding be kept constant? Tugged at by the pull of the earth, infected by the white stroke that engraved the book, furrowed, lines burned through it by hardship and torment and terror-unbalanced, brain-sick, at your last gasp on a rock in the sea, the pudding has boiled over and you are no worse than raving mad.' The microcosmic imagery, connecting the man to the rock to the universe, becomes a vast metaphor to convey the futility of man's sanity, of man's careful and calculated attempts to achieve salvation.

The 'gimmick' in *Pincher Martin* occurs in the final chapter. His body is washed ashore and the naval officer who comes to identify him points out that Martin couldn't have suffered long because he didn't even have time to kick off his seaboots. Supposedly, in the narrative itself, the first thing Martin did, before he even sighted the rock, was to kick his seaboots off. In other words, the final scene shows that the whole drama on the rock was but a momentary flash in Martin's mind. The dimension of time has been removed and all the microcosmic metaphor is but an instantaneous, apocalyptic vision. In the ultimate sense, this revelation enhances the microcosm, compresses all the issues into a single instant in time. But the revelation, in fact, makes the situation too complete, too contrived, seems to carry the development of the microcosm to the point of parodying itself. One can accept the struggle of forces on the rock as emblematic of a constant human struggle, but, when the dimension of time is removed, when the struggle is distilled to an instantaneous flash, one immediately thinks of parody in which the struggle was not significant at all. The 'gimmick', in this case, extends the technique, but so magnifies and exaggerates the extension that the novel ends by supplying its own parody.

In . . . *Free Fall*, Golding also deals with the limitation and the folly of the assumption that man can control his universe rationally, but, here, the futility of rationalism is not the central issue of the novel. The novel, anchored in social probability more securely than is any of the others, tells the story of Sammy Mountjoy who rose from the slums of Rotten Row to become a successful artist. Sammy, telling his own story, searches for the moment at which he lost his freedom, at which he made a crucial decision that inescapably hardened his natural propensity toward sin. The metaphor is Faustian: at what point and for what reason was this soul given over to Satan? Sammy, guilt-ridden, traces his career, looking for the point and the reason. He quickly dismisses the poverty of his background, his illegitimate birth, his youthful blasphemy against the church, his early membership in the Communist party – most of these were external and Sammy was essentially innocent then. He waives aside his seduction and subsequent desertion of the dependent Beatrice, his willingness to betray his comrades when a prisoner of war in Germany, his dishonesty – these were not causes, but effects, the patterns established by a man already irrevocably fallen. He examines his attraction to the rationalism preached by an early science teacher, but decides that this was not the cause, for, though the doctrine was shoddy and incomplete, the teacher himself was a man of principles deeper than those he avowed, and Sammy had always preferred the man to the doctrine. Finally, Sammy localises his loss of freedom in his early decision to pursue Beatrice at whatever cost. He had, while at school, drawn a picture of her and given it to one of his less talented friends to hand in as his own. The picture was highly praised; none of Sammy's other drawings received the recognition that this one did, and this one was publicly credited to someone else. Sammy kept trying, unsuccessfully, to draw Beatrice again. She then became an obsession for him; he had to track her down, pursue her, possess her, sacrifice everything in order to gain her. And this decision, taken as he left school, marks Sammy's loss of freedom. The decision, the willingness to sacrifice everything to achieve his aim, is an indication of human pride and egoism, the conscious human impulse to abandon concern for others, freedom of action, salvation itself, for the satisfaction of one's own end. Sammy relentlessly pursues and possesses Beatrice, overcoming her apathy and gentility by sheer energy and force. She does not satisfy him, for the appetite of human pride is endless, and he deserts her. Like Faust, Sammy loses his freedom when he is willing to stake everything on the satisfaction of his human pride.

At the end of the novel, when Sammy has discovered his sin, the reader suddenly learns that Beatrice has been in a mental institution ever since Sammy deserted her seven years earlier. Sammy visits her, but she will not speak to him and she urinates, in fright, on the floor when he tries to force her to acknowledge his existence. The doctor later tells him that Beatrice is incurable. When Sammy seeks to pin down just how guilty he is, the doctor replies: 'You probably tipped her over. But perhaps she would have tipped over anyway. Perhaps she would have tipped over a year earlier if you hadn't been there to give her something to think about. You may have given her an extra year of sanity and – whatever you did give her. You may have taken a lifetime of happiness away from her. Now you know the chances as accurately as a specialist.' Here, the 'gimmick', the final scene at the mental institution, both exaggerates and palliates the metaphorical structure of the novel. The fact that Beatrice is in an institution at all magnifies the external consequences of Sammy's sin and becomes, in Beatrice's unfortunate behavior, almost a parody of the damage caused by human pride. The novel shifts from Sammy's self-examination to the disastrous effect of his pride on others. After Sammy's sin is externalised, the doctor's sensible comment questions the possiblity of directly charging one person with the responsibility for another and, to some

measure, cuts down Sammy's guilt. But the novel was originally concerned with Sammy's loss of freedom, with this individual and interior issue, reflected by implication inside other
human beings. By making the issue exterior, the ending both
exaggerates and simplifies the description of the nature of man
involved, both softens and hedges concerning man's guilt. The
Faust legend loses much of its power if Faust is to be charged
with preaching sedition to his students or if Faust is to wonder
about his share of guilt when his students break church
windows. The final 'gimmick' in *Free Fall*, in making interior
issues exterior, changes some of the meaning, dissipates some of
the force and relevance, of the novel.

In each novel, the final 'gimmick' gives the novel a twist that, in
one way or another, palliates the force of the original metaphor.
It is almost as if, in each instance, Golding is backing down
from the implications of the metaphor itself, never really
contradicting the metaphor, but adding a twist that makes the
metaphor less sure, less permanently applicable. The
metaphors are steered away from what would seem to be their
relentless and inevitable conclusions, prevented, at the very
last moment, from hardening into the complete form of
allegory. In an aesthetic sense, one feels cheated at the end of a
Golding novel, tricked by a 'gimmick' that cuts down the force
and range of the metaphor, forced to look at the issues
presented more superficially, less universally, than he had
before. But, in another sense, each 'gimmick' provides a
qualification on the metaphor itself, widens the area of
perception as it undoubtedly lessens the force of the imaginative concept. If the adult world reduces the boys in *Lord of the
Flies*, is the depravity and brutality of human nature so
complete? How adequate is *Pincher Martin*'s microcosmic
synthesis, if it all flashes by in a second? Can Sammy Mountjoy,
living in a world that includes others, talking to them, sleeping
with them, helped by them, keep his guilt and the problem of
his freedom all to himself? Is the Faust legend an adequate
expression of the problems of contemporary man? All these
questions are implicit in the 'gimmicks' Golding uses. And the
'gimmicks', aesthetically unsatisfactory as they are, are quali-

fications on the universality of the metaphors, devices questioning the pretense that the metaphors contain complete truth.

Golding's metaphors can all be read as orthodox and traditional Christian statements about the nature of man. Each metaphor underlines man's depravity, pride, the futility of his reason. The novels are permeated with a sense of man's sin and guilt, and the images depict these qualities in conventional Christian terms. But the 'gimmicks' back down, to some extent, from the completeness, the finality, of the theologically orthodox statements. In an age when many writers view man's experience as disparate, impossible to codify, existential, Golding's metaphors suggest the reality, the permanence, of the traditional Christian explanation of the nature of man. The 'gimmicks', however, complicate the matter. As they dilute the aesthetic force of the traditional statement, so they simultaneously provide some concession to contemporary man's fear of generalised absolutes, to his existential attitude. This is not to suggest that Golding reverses his metaphors with these slender 'gimmicks', that the novels ultimately demonstrate the failure of the orthodox explanations. Rather, the 'gimmicks' indicate something of the complexity of contemporary experience, the difficulty in allowing a single, directed metaphor to convey all that man has to say about himself and his world. The metaphors still stand. In Golding's world, the orthodox Christian versions of man's depravity and limitations still convey a great deal that is relevant and permanent. But they don't convey everything. Palliation and parody may dissipate some of the force of Golding's metaphors, disturb their unity and mock their implicit presumption of completeness, seem to cheat by means of a clever switch at the end of the novel. Yet the palliation and parody, the effects of the 'gimmick', also indicate that Golding's world is wider, more complex, less easily contained by the orthodox implications of the metaphors, than seemed apparent at first. Aesthetic force itself can sometimes over-simplify.

SOURCE: essay in *Modern Fiction Studies*, VI (1960), pp. 145–52.

Peter Green   The World of William Golding   (1963)

Today, a century and a half after it first began to gather momentum, the Industrial Revolution remains the largest, most far-reaching, and least appreciated influence on all our lives. The physical effects it produced, and continues to produce, carry moral, social and spiritual implications which only now are we beginning to understand, and most of which we are powerless to alter. Essentially, what the Machine Age has meant in human terms is the by-passing of man's irrational, non-logical element. This is a vast over-simplification, but it contains a basic truth.

Most of the changes that have taken place during the last hundred years or so are, however improbably, interrelated; they share a common causality. The growth of an urban industrial society, the decay of traditional religious fundamentalism, the dissemination of scientific method; moral uncertainty, technological advance, the artificial retreat to primitivism, the flourishing neuroses which facilitated the development of psychology and psychiatry; automation, logical positivism, thermo-nuclear deterrents, Admass, political propaganda, Billy Graham, horror comics, science fiction, rock 'n roll, angst, the death-wish, sexual frustration or hysteria: one pattern binds them all together.

This needs further explanation in historical terms. The more obvious by-products of the Industrial Revolution have become textbook truisms; but historians are seldom interested in following up their conclusions in terms of the individual. We know that our society has become urbanised, that labour is constantly draining from the country to the town. We are by no means so certain what this means in its overall context. We are not sure how *we* are affected by the breakdown of rural culture; we cannot judge the long-term effects of city life. Things have moved too fast for us. Man's metabolism changes slowly by nature; and in a century it has had to adapt itself more than in the previous thirty thousand years.

Several factors have combined to offer us a comforting, but ultimately dangerous, protection. Foremost among these has been the notion that science could, in some mysterious way, be made a substitute for religion. It is no coincidence that such a large proportion of scientists are, or used to be, Marxists. Man is a creature for whom patterns are essential; and when T. H. Huxley and his successors destroyed the absolute sanctity of traditional Christianity, what was more natural than that the iconoclasts should themselves set up a new (if secular) Church? Reason was their sovereign god; reason could solve all the problems of the universe. The soul was a fiction, emotions could be rationalised in terms of hormones. God (to revive the old Voltairean gibe) was a Job's Comforter created by man in his own narcissistic image.

The consequences of this strangely unilateral creed were grave in the extreme: but then, most human attempts to upset the balance of nature tend to be calamitous. What happened, in effect, was that half of human nature – the emotional, instinctive, irrational element, the back rather than the front of the mind – was treated simply as if it did not exist. There is a popular delusion among scientists, which they share, incidentally, with primitive witch-doctors, that by naming a thing they render it harmless. Logic stuck its labels on the universe, and analogies from the natural sciences multiplied thick and fast. Natural selection was used to justify racial persecution; the notion of evolution became transformed into Wellsian social progressivism. The smug religious superiority of the early Victorians gave place to the smug scientific superiority of the early anthropologist. The universe was as tidy and as comprehensible, for a few years, as the Crystal Palace.

For a few years, but no longer. Violent suppression tends to breed violent reaction; and soon the air was thick with cries of 'back to the Land', while urban radicals preached a new urban egalitarianism. Neuroses grew and proliferated alarmingly. It was the functional scientific attitude to sex no less than Puritan repression or industrial materialism which produced the mere casual concupiscence which both D. H.

Lawrence and Mr Eliot attacked. Reason could stick new labels on the emotions; but it could neither argue nor legislate them out of existence. It would rationalise God by discussing religion in terms of personal psychology; but God (under whatever name) remained. And of course, above all, reason could rationalise its own motives; it seldom occurs to any scientist to admit that his tenets are no less dogmatic than those of Christianity, and that his logical inferences normally rest on a solid bedrock of emotional prejudice. He has a name and a label for everything.

This may seem a long, perhaps an irrelevant, introduction to William Golding's work: but it is, I think, indispensable if we are to understand that work fully. 'His job', Golding once wrote of the novelist, 'is to scrape the labels off things, to take nothing for granted, to show the irrational where it exists.' The novels he has so far published [i.e., to 1960 – Ed.]* demonstrate this process in action. Man, Golding is saying, has grown away both from nature and himself. He is protected from reality not only by city life, labour-saving devices, canned food, electric light, running water, daily papers, and indifference to the seasons, but also by the spiritual blindness which such conditions breed. He is cushioned in smugness; he has become his own God. Nothing can touch him. Golding has made it his task to break down these false illusions: his creed is that of the Delphic Oracle, *Know Yourself*. He has put it on record that he 'is making statements all the time about John Smith, Twentieth Century citizen. Writing about schoolboys, Neanderthalers and dead sailors appears to him to be a simple means of turning a light on contemporary human nature. He believes the only hope for humanity is self-knowledge, attained and practised by the individual.' In an interview for *Books and Art* [March 1958] he also made it clear that the basic problem of modern humanity, in his view, was that of learning to live fearlessly with the natural chaos of existence, without forcing artifical

---

* Though published in 1963, Peter Green's essay was first prepared for a lecture delivered in 1960 [Ed.]

patterns on it. To his interviewer he asserted: 'The difference between being alive and being an inorganic substance is just the proliferation of experience, this absence of pattern.'

In an earlier article[1] he had also clarified his position as a novelist with regard to political 'involvement' and modern scientific discoveries:

Current affairs [he wrote] are only expressions of the basic human condition where his [the novelist's] true business lies. If he has a serious, an Aeschylean, preoccupation with the human tragedy, that is only to say that he is committed to looking for the root of the disease instead of describing the symptoms. I can't help feeling that critics of this Aeschylean outlook are those who think they have an easy answer to all problems simply because they have never looked further than the rash appearing on the skin. They want Gulliver to declare himself for one end or other of the egg.

As for awareness of recent discoveries in biology, astronomy and psychology, it is a necessary part of any mind's equipment. . . . [But] to be aware of discoveries need not mean that we over-rate their importance – need not mean that we should picture our flesh under the electron microscope when our real job is to show it *sub specie aeternitatis*. . . .

Golding, in fact, is, primarily, a religious novelist: his central theme is not the relationship of man to man (which I suspect he considers of secondary importance) but the relationship of man, the individual, to the universe; and through the universe, to God. He is going back behind our distracting modern clutter of physical impedimenta to search for basic truths that have been obscured by material progress. He is a spiritual cosmologist.

Any attentive reader of his novels published [so far] will perceive at once that their symbolism is, in essence, theological. Both *Lord of the Flies* and *The Inheritors* are concerned with the primal loss of innocence. *The Inheritors*, indeed, can be read as an anthropological allegory of the Fall, with Lok and Fa as a prelapsarian Adam and Eve. *Pincher Martin*, as the last chapter proves, explicitly concerns the sufferings of a dead man who has created his own Purgatory. It is a moral axiom of Golding's that Man, and Man alone, introduced evil into the world: a view which is hardly separable from the doctrine of Original Sin. This is suggestive. To a critic who suggested that good was equally an exclusive human concept, he replied: 'Good can look after itself. Evil is the problem.' This attitude suggests both the emotional strength of his work and the intellectual paradox underlying it. He wants to scrape off the labels, to destroy artificial patterns. He represents himself, theologically, as what used to be loosely termed a Deist; and yet the whole moral framework of his novels is conceived in terms of traditional Christian symbolism.

Nevertheless, the paradox, on closer thought, can be resolved. In the first place, a novelist with a fundamental moral problem to communicate must be understood by his audience; and to be understood he must use symbols which are familiar and can be readily apprehended, preferably those that have sunk into the archetypal consciousness of European readers. Secondly, Golding is a man in search of cosmological truth; and it might well be argued that – as he himself has often proclaimed in a slightly different context – the names, the labels, do not matter. It is only the ultimate reality that counts, and must at all costs be communicated.

Having established the background, let us now consider the four novels separately, in the order of their appearance.

Lord of the Flies was published in 1954, and acclaimed, though somewhat uneasily, by English critics. The main outline of the plot is by now well known. Somewhere an atomic war is raging (the novel is, ironically, set in the future), and a plane-load of schoolboys crashes on a deserted tropical island in the Pacific. There are palm-trees, sandy beaches, a lagoon to swim in, plentiful ripe fruit; the setting is perfect for the re-enactment of that perennial and highly charged boyhood myth, which found its most famous expression in R. M. Ballantyne's *The Coral Island* – life, primitive life, unhampered by pettifogging, over-civilised, authoritarian adults.

Since Golding's explicit purpose is to stand the Ballantyne myth on its head – in ways *Lord of the Flies* deliberately parodies the earlier book – it is instructive to re-read *The Coral Island*, with this in mind. It was published . . . in 1858, at the high tide of Victorian self-confidence, and is permeated with smug national complacency, synthetic missionary fervour, and a kind of paralysing condescension which could only blossom in a safe, stable, unreflecting society. The boys are pint-sized adults, whose priggish conversation is spattered with semi-colons. The social and moral scale of things is clearly deline-ated: Britons come at the top of it, savages and pigs at the bottom. The boys kill pigs with the same unthinking self-assurance they employ to bully the natives into Christianity, or read them a moral lecture on the sin of cannibalism. The book ends with the burning of the false gods of Mango, and then hurrah for dear old England. Nothing, moreover, is allowed to disrupt the emotional unity of the three boys, Jack, Ralph and Peterkin. 'There was, indeed', Ballantyne wrote, in a particu-larly mawkish moment, 'no note of discord whatever in the symphony we played together on that sweet Coral Island; and I am now persuaded that this was owing to our having been all tuned to the same key, namely, that of *love!*'

Now it is easy enough to see how a novelist armed with the findings of Frazer, Freud and Piaget could turn this rubbishy myth inside out. *A High Wind in Jamaica* pointed the way; a century of social change lies between Ballantyne's and Golding's position. Mr V. S. Pritchett, writing in the *New Statesman*, both summarised this development and hinted at its further implications [see Part Two, above]. Golding's children, then, are isolated on their desert island for a specific spiritual experiment, much as a scientist might isolate a culture in a Petri dish; and their behaviour must be considered in the light of their author's known convictions.

At one level – and this is the aspect of the book which most critics have emphasised – *Lord of the Flies* portrays a gradual reversion to the most primitive and bloodthirsty savagery. To begin with the children impose 'civilised' standards of conduct on their small community. As Jack observes, in a recognisable parody of Ballantyne: 'We've got to have rules and obey them. After all, we're not savages. We're English; and the English are best at everything. So we've got to do the right things.' They elect a leader, Ralph. They have a meeting-place for discussion, and a conch-shell to summon them. This conch also becomes a symbol of rational behaviour; no one may speak unless he is holding it. And here, already, the percipient reader gets his first twinge of uneasiness, remembering that a similar habit prevailed among Homer's heroes. Just as the embryo in the womb recapitulates evolutionary development, so these young boys are slipping back on the path that leads to primitivism.

And so it turns out. Gradually, conditions being right for it, the shibboleths of twentieth-century civilisation are erased with appalling ease from these middle-class boys' minds. First come irrational fears: of imaginary monsters and the numinous unknown. There is a feeling of 'something behind you all the time in the jungle'. Then the boys split into two groups: the hunters, and those struggling to retain their civilised standards. The hunters, their initial squeamishness lost, revel in the blood-lust induced by pig-sticking. They daub their faces with coloured clay: Jack, their leader, is 'safe from shame or self-consciousness behind the mask of his paint'. Then comes the inevitable ritual *mimesis: 'Kill the pig!'* they howl, dancing round its reeking, dismembered corpse. *'Cut his throat! Kill the pig! Bash him in!'* It is only a matter of time before their collective anger turns against a human victim.

'Which is better?' cries Ralph in desperation: 'law and rescue, or hunting and breaking things up?' There is no doubt which Jack will choose: not 'the world of longing and baffled commonsense', but 'the brilliant world of hunting, tactics, fierce exhilaration, skill'. It is characteristic of the hunters that they loathe and despise those who will not join them. Two of these, Piggy and Simon, are murdered; the third, Ralph himself, is hunted across the island, and only saved by the opportune arrival of a Royal Navy landing-party. (The last episode, incidentally, allows the author to bang his point home with superb irony. 'I should have thought', remarks the hearty officer who stumbles on the survivors, 'I should have thought that a pack of British boys – you're all British aren't you? – would have been able to put up a better show than that – I mean –' and trails away into incoherence, only rallying to add, with hopeful optimism: 'Jolly good show. Like the Coral Island.')

But behind this main narrative structure, as always in Golding's work, we find more universal moral implications. What Ralph weeps for, on the last page, is 'the end of innocence, the darkness of man's heart'. Piggy is more than a fat, asthmatic, coddled, myopic, stubbornly sensible Cockney:

he is the voice of sanity personified, a Promethean symbol. It is his thick-lensed spectacles which are used to light the vital signal-fire, and are later stolen by the hunters. He will have no truck with the group-consciousness, but remains embarrassingly individual; and because of this he is killed. Seen in this sense, the book reveals a terrifying microcosm of political totalitarianism. The experiment acquires unexpected relevance to the whole human condition.

With Simon we are at a deeper level still. Simon – we have Golding's own word for it – is a saint, mystic and clairvoyant. It is Simon, and Simon alone, who sees the others' fear and superstition for what they are. This point is made by the use of two very explicit symbols: the Beast, and the Lord of the Flies himself.

The Beast, to begin with, is nothing more than a focal point for the boys' vague, inarticulate, archaic fears. 'What I mean is', stammers Simon (and is shouted down for his pains), 'maybe it's only us': he is, as Golding puts it, 'inarticulate in his effort to express mankind's essential illness'. Later the Beast is given a spurious reality: the corpse of an airman, still harnessed to its parachute, drifts down from some aerial battle on to the beacon hill at the top of the island. Two children see it in the dark, and instantly the myth of terror is established. But Simon, again, is incredulous: 'however Simon thought of the beast, there rose before his inward sight the picture of a human at once heroic and sick.'

Meanwhile Jack, whose instinct tells him the Beast must be placated, erects a pole in the forest with a pig's head stuck on top of it as an offering. Simon, walking alone, stumbles on this totemic emblem, buzzing with flies, and instantly, instinctively, knows it for what it is. The more sophisticated reader quickly works out the equation. Baalzebub was the Philistine Lord of Flies; the Jews transmuted his name to mean Lord of Dung or Filth; by the time of the New Testament he was Lord of the Devils, a generalised Satan. It is this potent deity with whom Simon has his strange conversation in the jungle:

Simon's head was tilted slightly up. His eyes could not break away and the Lord of the Flies hung in space before him.

'What are you doing out here all alone? Aren't you afraid of me?'
Simon shook.
'There isn't anyone to help you. Only me. And I'm the Beast.'
Simon's mouth laboured, brought forth audible words.
'Pig's head on a stick.'
'Fancy thinking the Beast was something you could hunt and kill!' said the
head. For a moment or two the forest and all the other dimly appreciated
places echoed with the parody of laughter. 'You knew, didn't you? I'm part of
you. Close, close, close! I'm the reason why it's no go? Why things are what
they are?'

In other words, it is man who creates his own hell, his own
devils; the evil is in him. As John Peter put it: 'Beelzebub, Lord
of the Flies, is Roger and Jack and you and I, ready to declare
himself as soon as we permit him to.' [Peter's essay is included
in Part Two, above – Ed.]

Armed with this self-knowledge, Simon climbs the hill and
sees the rotting corpse for what it is; he cuts it adrift and lets the
wind carry it, still in its parachute, out to sea. Then, eager to tell
the healing truth, he starts off down to the shore: 'the beast was
harmless and horrible; and the news must reach the others as
soon as possible'. But the frenzied hunters will not listen to him:
they tear him limb from limb in a ritual orgy, while he is still
shrieking about a dead man up on the hill. Man, Golding seems
to be saying, cherishes his guilt, his fears, his taboos, and will
crucify any saint or redeemer who offers to relieve him of his
burden by telling the simple truth. There is a horrible symbolic
appropriateness about the corpse itself: the nameless devil and
its victims are identical. Evil is ineradicable: the Earthly
Paradise is a delusion. Man's heart is dark, and no innocence
lives beneath the sun; or if it does, it must, inevitably, suffer and
die as Piggy and Simon died, their wisdom and virtue destroyed
by the Beast's devotees.

Now from the reviews which *Lord of the Flies* received on
publication it is plain that few critics or readers worked out its
deeper implications consciously. All recognised its power; but
it reached them in the same way as a good poem, through direct
emotional apprehension. Like any good propagandist, Mr
Golding slipped a fast one on his audience: he got beneath their
rational guard. At the same time, there was a general question

in the air: what in the world (or out of it) would he do next? Had he landed himself in a creative cul-de-sac?

A year later all such doubts were dispelled by the publication of *The Inheritors*. Indeed, it almost looked as though this unpredictable author had deliberately set himself an impossible task. A novel about Neanderthal Man? It would either be incomprehensible or a joke. But it was not: it was a more brilliant *tour de force* than *Lord of the Flies*, and demonstrated with even greater clarity Golding's extraordinary gift for identifying himself, in an empathic sense, with beings totally beyond the normal range of human creative awareness.

Once again, Golding set himself the task of standing a traditional *idée reçue* on its head. This time he moved on a little, from an old complacency to a new one. In *Lord of the Flies* he attacked the moral self-satisfaction of Victorian society. In *The Inheritors* he challenged its direct successor, the smugly superior progressivism of evolutionary science. No one single man is more closely associated with this movement in the popular mind than H. G. Wells; and it was from Wells's *Outline of History*, accordingly, that Golding took his epigraph, where Neanderthal Man is patronisingly described as an inferior creature who probably suggested the cannibalistic ogre of folk-tale. There is little doubt that he also had in mind Wells's own story of the meeting of Neanderthal Man and *homo sapiens*, *The Grisly Folk*. In this tale all Wells's sympathies, as we might expect, are with *homo sapiens*, humanity, achievement, discovery, progress. The Neanderthalers are huge, half-witted, cruel monsters: one of them steals a human child, and Wells exults in their hunting down and ultimate destruction.

Golding exactly reverses this concept. Here it is the Neanderthalers who are creatures of primal innocence: it is the new men, and they alone, who introduce guilt, crime, suffering and conscious ambition into the world. Professor Kermode has summed up the major theme admirably: 'The price of human consciousness, of technical and linguistic power', he writes, 'is guilt. . . . The intellectual superiority which enables this victory is precisely measured by the cruelty and guilt invented in the process. Man, who cooks, makes drawings, alcohol and love, can think; he replaces with language that picture-dialect, guiltless of all abstracting, which the victim used, and which is found in *homo sapiens* only in certain pathological conditions.'[2] It at once becomes clear that there is a close thematic connexion between *The Inheritors* and *Lord of the Flies*: Mr Golding has simply set up a different working model to illustrate the eternal human verities from a new angle. Again it is humanity, and humanity alone, that generates evil; and when the new men triumph, Lok, the Neanderthaler, weeps as Ralph wept, for the corruption and end of innocence.

But what most immediately astonishes and impresses any reader of *The Inheritors* is its incredible atmosphere of immediacy and realism. 'The grisly folk', Wells wrote – and what better illustrates his entrenched progressivist dogma? – 'we cannot begin to understand. We cannot conceive in our different minds the strange ideas that chased one another through those queerly shaped brains. As well might we try to dream and feel as a gorilla dreams and feels.' *The Inheritors* gives this statement the lie direct. Striking a superb technical balance between external comment (which permits intellectual glossing) and internal impressionism, Mr Golding projects a wholly convincing recreation of the Neanderthaler's cloudy, static, non-abstract awareness of life. This is a world where past and future are both little more than extensions of the present; where ideas and communication are a series of separate 'pictures', like a lantern-lecture; where neither action nor its corollary, speech, contains any subordinate clauses.

Coupled with Golding's intense awareness of the natural world, organic or inorganic (he seems to see each separate rock, tree, beast, or fish as Aldous Huxley saw jewels under the influence of mescalin), this insight into his Neanderthalers' minds enables him to sustain the sense of actuality throughout *The Inheritors*. Skilfully he introduces his essential clues: the first whiff of the unknown creature on the wind; the sense of kinship with earth; the primal cosmogony; the badness of killing earth's children; at last the contact with the new men.

Till the last chapter we see *homo sapiens* entirely from the viewpoint of the Neanderthaler. We share Lok's puzzlement at their incomprehensible appearance and habits: 'they were people', he decides, 'without pictures in their heads.' When one of them shoots a poisoned arrow at him, Lok 'had a confused idea that someone was trying to give him a present.' By this method Golding jolts us out of our unthinking assumptions, forces us to re-examine what hitherto we had taken for granted. All primary human activities are filtered through the polarised lens of Lok's unfamiliarity: sympathetic hunting magic, ritual mimesis (the magician in a stag's head), the use of artefacts such as dug-out canoes; murder; religious heave-offerings, intoxication, the conscious and deliberate pursuit of pleasure in the act of love. Gradually, as he and Fa spy on these strange, alien creatures, they too are corrupted. Experience breeds awareness. They drink the alcoholic mead and feel identification with the new folk, only to wake and vomit afterwards. Lok looks at Fa with new eyes; and he also, in a brilliantly suggested passage, stumbles on the notion of 'likeness': dimly we sense him reaching forward to the simile, the metaphor, the first stirrings of poetry, the magic neutralisation by naming: 'Likeness could grasp the white-faced hunters with a hand, could put them into the world where they were thinkable and not a random and unrelated irruption.'

Again the identification with *Lord of the Flies* becomes apparent. These new, bony-faced creatures, Tuami and the rest, hunting, performing magic, placating their devils – what are they but Jack and Roger reincarnate in the backwardness of time? 'They have gone over us like a hollow log', cries Lok in his agony. 'They are like a winter.' From the beginning their triumph is inevitable; with a last flick of malice at Wells, Golding ends his story by making the New Men abduct a Neanderthal baby. Nothing is solved; corruption is complete; evil and knowledge have triumphed.

As I suggested earlier, *The Inheritors* can be read as an allegory, at one level, of the Fall; and since Golding himself insists that Lok is a prelapsarian, this is almost certainly how he intended it. Lok and Fa thus become anthropological analogues of Adam and Eve; but it is Man himself whom Golding identifies with the Serpent, and who tempts Lok to eat of the Tree of Knowledge. This blazingly heretical version of the Paradisal legend, again, does not seem to have been consciously appreciated by most critics; but its latent effect, I fancy, was considerable. One extremely intelligent Catholic novelist flatly refused to review the book; it is not hard to see why.

The Inheritors, like all successful works of art, is self-contained: it stands or falls without reference to its historical validity. On the other hand, since Golding knows a great deal about anthropology, and has been a life-long amateur archaeologist, it is interesting to see whether or not he has reshaped Neanderthal Man to suit his particular moral purpose. In fact he has: no mention is made of their undoubted cannibalism, or primitive tool-making, or glimmerings of magic; and consequently their primal innocence is clearly over-emphasised.[3] Recently, too, the discovery of a human skeleton *twelve million years old* in an Italian lignite mine has meant the total revision of anthropological prehistory. Neanderthal Man is no longer *homo sapiens'* precursor, but over many thousands of years his contemporary; perhaps an aberrant mutation. While this new evidence does not in any way impair the creative achievement of *The Inheritors*, it does give an unexpected and unfortunate twist to its underlying symbolism.

Between *The Inheritors* and his next novel, *Pincher Martin*, Golding wrote, unexpectedly, a short satirical *novella*, *Envoy Extraordinary*, later dramatised as *The Brass Butterfly*. To most readers this was merely a welcome proof that the author, after all, had a sense of humour. The plot has close affinities with 'The Rewards of Industry', a story in Richard Garnett's *The Twilight of the Gods*; it concerns a Greek inventor, Phanocles, who comes to the court of an unspecified but highly decadent Roman Emperor with five premature inventions: the steamship, gunpowder, printing, the compass, and the pressure cooker. After a demonstration of the disastrous effects which steam and explosives can have on human society, Phanocles is hurried off to China, out of the way, leaving the Emperor with the pressure cooker – the most Promethean discovery of them all.

Both the *novella* and the play (which differ in significant details) are an attack on the scientific temperament and the abuse of scientific knowledge. 'Confused, illogical, and extremely hubristic', the Emperor remarks of Phanocles's pretensions, and goes on: 'I said you are hubristic. You are also selfish. You are alone in your universe with natural law and people are an interruption, an intrusion. . . . Your single-minded and devoted selfishness, your royal preoccupation with the only thing that can interest you, could go near to wiping life off the earth as I wipe the bloom from this grape.' Once again, Golding has indissolubly linked the concepts of human knowledge and human evil. But now we understand, retrospectively, that an additional element has been present throughout his work: the Prometheus myth. Man the maker, the inventor, the builder must suffer for his knowledge. Like Piggy, he has stolen fire from heaven. Like Lok, he has eaten the forbidden fruit. Expulsion from Paradise is only the beginning; it leads by slow degrees to the purgatorial Caucasian rock, the eagle tearing endlessly at his vitals. So the scene is set for the third, Aeschylean, novel: *Pincher Martin*.

It is essential, right from the beginning, to make it quite clear what *Pincher Martin* is about. Most critics, with a few honourable exceptions, though they lauded the book to the skies, completely missed its point. In particular, they objected to what was generally described as the 'trick ending'. The entire novel, you will remember, has concerned a naval lieutenant's desperate efforts, after being torpedoed, to survive, alone, on Rockall. In the first chapter he kicks off his sea-boots to avoid drowning. On the last page, when his corpse is washed ashore, it is made clear that he was drowned *before* he had time to kick them off. What is the explanation?

'The essential point', John Peter wrote in *Kenyon Review*, 'is that this is a story about a dead man. . . .' [see his essay above – Ed.] The existence he enjoys is a figment of his own will only, and in the most secret recesses of his being he remains horrifiedly aware of its unreality. Mr W. J. Harvey, echoing this interpretation, adds that 'the whole action of the novel takes place in the few seconds of his actual drowning or perhaps in some after-death state in which he is given the chance to choose salvation or damnation'.[4] Golding himself is even more explicit: 'Pincher', he writes, 'is simply in hell. The whole of *Pincher Martin* is Pincher's *post mortem* experience of himself ("Nothing burns in hell but the self").' 'Myself am Hell': 'Why, this is Hell, nor am I out of it.' From Marlowe to Blake, from Milton to Sartre, echoes of Pincher's self-inflicted purgatory come crowding to the mind.

Now Mr Golding makes it quite clear that Pincher's struggle for survival is not intended to be seen as heroic, but rather as egotistical, in the Hobbesian sense. He is clinging with fierce desperation to his own small, mean pattern of existence. He refuses to acknowledge the cosmic chaos of death. Yet, paradoxically enough, it is just at this point that Pincher – like Milton's Satan – breaks away from his creator's original intention. However despicable his character – and Mr Golding, as we shall see in a moment, makes him out a classic four-letter man – he nevertheless compels our admiring respect for his epic, unyielding struggle in the face of overwhelming odds. He feeds off limpets and sea-anemones. He improvises shelter, builds a cairn to attract ships, makes a huge sos sign out of seaweed in the hope that a passing aircraft will spot it. He pits three thousand years of human knowledge, intelligence and will-power against the blind forces of nature. 'I am busy surviving', he remarks to himself. 'I am netting down this rock with names and taming it. Some people would be incapable of understanding the importance of that. What is given a name is given a seal, a chain. If this rock tries to adapt me to its ways I will refuse and adapt it to mine. I will impose my routine on it, my geography. I will tie it down with names.'

Indeed, Christopher Martin is more than an individual sailor, suffering on a specific rock: he is a mythic symbol of man's steadfast endurance. He is the much-travelled, long-enduring, crafty Odysseus, spewing the salt water from his lungs, battered yet surviving. He is Ajax defying the lightning. 'Why drag in good and evil', he cries, 'when the serpent lies coiled in my own body? . . . I am Atlas. I am Prometheus.' He is Lear in his madness and defiant to the end. He sums up every quality that distinguishes man from the beasts.

To offset this Mr Golding presents Pincher, in a series of flashbacks, as one of the nastiest characters ever to appear in fiction. Like Phlebas [the Phoenician], he passes 'the stages of his age and youth entering the whirlpool', and reveals himself as an adulterer, a homosexual, a thief, a rapist, and a would-be murderer. Here is how one of his peacetime friends, an actor like himself, describes him: 'This painted bastard here takes anything he can lay his hands on. . . . He takes the best part, the best seat, the most money, the best notice, the best woman. He was born with his mouth and his flies open and both hands out to grab. He's a cosmic case of the bugger who gets his penny and someone else's bun.' For the purposes of Mr Golding's allegory he has to be: if he were a good man, or even *l'homme moyen sensuel*, he would never have created this hell for himself in the first place.

'Like a dead man!' he exclaims at one point; and of course he *is* dead. Occasionally his imagination makes a mistake. He sees a red lobster swimming, scales a cliff by using limpets as suckers, forgets that guano is insoluble in water. The clue to his purgatorial experience is to be found in his exchanges with Nathaniel, again the innocent, saintly fool, who is simply Simon grown up. 'Take us as we are now', Nathaniel tells him, 'and heaven would be sheer negation . . . a sort of black lightning destroying everything that we call life.' What Pincher lacks is 'the technique of dying into heaven'; he adamantly refuses to admit the validity of spiritual experience, which Golding himself treats always 'as factual, not illusion'. When God appears to Pincher at the novel's apocalyptic climax, in the guise of the Old Man of the Sea, Pincher cries out: 'You are a projection of my mind. . . . I have created you and I can create my own heaven.' 'You have created it', the Old Man replies, with sombre irony. But even then Pincher stands fast. 'I spit on your comparison', he shrieks, as the black lightning plays about him; and his last words are: 'I shit on your heaven.'

This novel suggests the limitations as well as the possibilities of Golding's creative method. Nathaniel, as Professor Kermode pointed out, tells Prometheus-Pincher 'that evil is human' (which we know) 'and would vanish if the mind could alter its theme' – both of which premises seem highly arguable. *Au fond*,

Golding is a religious mystic, for whom the bulk of mankind is fiercely repellent, and in whose eyes only the saint or the prelapsarian – Simon, Lok, Nathaniel – can justify human existence. (Golding never, we may note – except in the doubtful case of Nathaniel and Mary – portrays a full emotional relationship between a man and a woman. It is not accident, one feels, that the mysterious, glamorous Euphrosyne of *Envoy Extraordinary* turns out in the end to have a hare-lip. This touch seems to have been too much for the producer of *The Brass Butterfly*, who removed the hare-lip and substituted a romantic affair with the Emperor's grandson.) This has some curious consequences. In the first place, it virtually excludes the normal range of human relationships which the novel covers. As Mr Harvey observed, Golding's imagination has always worked at a fair remove from the full body of human life. Only in *Pincher Martin* – and then only by means of flashbacks – is this rule broken; and here, so loathsome is the glimpse given of man's social behaviour, one returns to the bare wind-swept rock with a sigh of relief.

After the publication of *Pincher Martin*, Golding was asked, in an interview, what he now aimed to achieve. 'This time', he stated in reply, 'I want to show the patternlessness of life before we impose our patterns on it.' This was a local last step for him to contemplate, and one which hinted broadly at the creative impasse with which he was confronted. It was becoming increasingly difficult for him either to come to terms with humanity, or to ignore it. In the event, however, this new novel, *Free Fall*, avoids the amoebic paradox suggested by his own prophecy, and falls into a more normal pattern of development: normal, that is, for Golding. In the title itself we can at once recognise his two overriding themes, the perennial conflict. Man is doomed by Original Sin, and Fall is a reality. Yet the will remains free: self-destruction is a matter of choice. Once again Golding is exploring the two counterposed worlds of human awareness – the physical universe and the metaphysical, the worlds of Science and God.

This universal moral conflict is crystallised internally, in the mind of one Man, Sammy Mountjoy, an English artist. For the first time Golding is presenting us with first-person narrative; and in Sammy we have exactly the type of *l'homme moyen sensuel* which we missed in Pincher. Structurally the two novels must be bracketed together: both use the same system of flashbacks to unite and give depth to the perspective of a single vision, and both depend on the use of delayed shock-treatment. Only on the last line do we realise fully that Pincher is dead; only half-way through *Free Fall* do we become aware that Sammy's present predicament – at the time of thinking, as it were – is that of a POW officer under interrogation in a Nazi concentration camp during the war. His interrogator, a coldly clever academic psychologist, is applying various pressures in order to make him betray his comrades' escape-plans. What we are hearing is Sammy's *apologia pro vita sua*, his frantic autobiographical search for the incidents which, in the past, made him take one moral decision rather than another, his corrosive fear of spiritual bankruptcy. Has he, in fact, the inner resources necessary to hold out against his tormentor?

The web of memory shuttles to and fro: where was the failure, the wrong turning? Was it in the Kentish slum-tenement where he lived with his huge, boozy, warm-hearted slattern of a mother? Or later, at school, fumbling through the thickset, glimmering hedges of adolescence? Not here, he cries silently, not here. Did Miss Pringle, the frustrated religious puritan, turn me against her God because she was mean and cruel, just as old Nick Shales, that devoted teacher and scientist, drew me with the paradoxical love that irradiated his material world? When did I lose my freedom? By what act, what choice, what suffering?

It is Beatrice who offers the clue, and hints at the Dantean symbolism underlying so much of Golding's work. Sammy's own name, Mountjoy, suggests the Paradisal Mountain: if *Pincher Martin* is Golding's *Purgatorio*, *Free Fall* is his tragically marred *Paradiso*. Beatrice was the child whom Sammy tried to draw, the girl with the light of Paradise round her brow. Golding himself says of her:

But where Dante, presented with a coherent cosmos, was able to fit her into it, Sammy's confused cosmos ended by putting her through the whole mill of seduction – a scientific, rationalistic approach, so to speak, so that Beatrice who took Dante up to the vision of God becomes a clog to Sammy and a skeleton in his cupboard.

Sammy is responding, as he must, to the muddled, broken cosmos which is his inheritance; and Beatrice, abandoned, an ugly, incontinent, mindless wreck, is the cross he must bear. It is in solitary prison confinement, alone in a dark room, that he comes through to the truth – the same truth which Simon discovered in *Lord of the Flies* – that all terror, fear, despair are both of the human mind, and the human mind alone. The horrible Poe-like cell is revealed as an ordinary broom-cupboard; the fragment of cold, dead flesh is an abandoned floor cloth; the diabolical psychologist who investigated Sammy's past 'does not', the Camp Commandment apologetically explains, 'know about peoples'. And on this ironic note, with Sammy's burden of guilt clarified if not alleviated, the novel ends.

Or rather, as with all Golding's novels, begins. *In my end is my beginning*. From the cell Sammy cried *de profundis*, to the God in whom he could not completely believe; and the cell door opened, the drab prison camp outside was transmuted in Traherne-like splendour, Sammy had the Pentecostal vision and saw his companions walking in their glory like Kings of Egypt. And this tremendous experience at once swings us back to the opening pages of the book: indeed, to its opening paragraph. . . .

This, as Ian Gregor and Mark Kinkead-Weekes have pointed out, in a penetrating though perhaps too wholly defensive article,[5] contains the whole subsequent essence of the novel in miniature. Here are the torn and conflicting halves of Sammy's world and self: body and spirit, faith and pragmatism, Paradise Hill and the Mount of Venus. But it is only *after* the transfiguring experience in his prison cell that Sammy as narrator, and we as readers, can look back and fit the pieces of the puzzle together. (Yet Mr Golding always plays fair: there are plenty of 'hints and guesses, hints followed by guesses' for those who care to see them. A whole article could be written on his symbolic names, with their wealth of associative allusiveness: Christopher Martin, Christopher the Christ-bearer who becomes 'Pincher', the grasping egotist; or Sammy

Mountjoy, who is not only an inhabitant of the Paradisal Mountain, but the Infant Samuel and, in another sense, the sex-obsessed devotee of the Mons Veneris.) Finally and most important, it is only in this new novel that Mr Golding's perennial Everyman, astride the ages, at last brings himself to accept. Pincher died blaspheming; Sammy cries for help out of the depths of his uncertainty.

William Golding demands – insistently demands – to be judged by the very highest standards, both aesthetic and moral. On this level his new novel is a flawed masterpiece, the inordinately ambitious work of an indisputable genius just missing the centre of the target. Technically, *Free Fall* buckles a little here and there beneath its cumulative weight of symbolism and flashback, the latter occasionally achieving a probably unintentional ambiguity. For example: does the terrible asylum reunion with Beatrice take place in fact, after the war, or is it merely the creation of Sammy's imprisoned mind, the flash of tortured self-knowledge? Here and there, too, the writing, normally so objective and crystalline, blurs a little, as though from sheer intensity of desire to express the inexpressible. The twin problem of loneliness and communication dogs Sammy, as it has always dogged his creator:

> It is the unnameable, unfathomable and invisible darkness that sits at the centre of him, always awake, always different from what you believe it to be, always thinking and feeling what you can never know it thinks and feels, that hopes hopelessly to understand and to be understood. Our loneliness is the loneliness not of the cell or the castaway; it is the loneliness of that dark thing that sees as at the atom furnace by reflection, feels by remote control and hears only words phoned out to it in a foreign tongue. To communicate is our passion and our despair.

But for moral sincerity and cosmic splendour of vision this novel towers above most contemporary fiction.

It is no accident that the term of praise most often used to describe Golding's work is 'a *tour de force*'. In each novel he has created special conditions – a desert island, a prehistoric wilderness, a lonely rock, a prison cell – where he could experiment in isolation, without external influence. In each, again, he has chosen his characters so as to exclude the exploration of full adult relationships: pre-adolescent boys, inarticulate Neanderthalers, a shipwrecked sailor who is dead into the bargain and therefore doubly *hors concours*. With Sammy Mountjoy we see him beginning, with immense effort, to struggle free of this isolating tendency. Sammy speaks for himself, and therefore, inevitably, with a degree of self-justification as well as guilty self-reproach. He is asking questions, not imposing patterns; shaking the bars of his cage, challenging his own inner convictions. Sammy, the contemporary, fumbling, destructive, yet essentially well-meaning hedonist – Sammy the visionary, the artist, who loves his coarse Welsh wife with a ferocious tenderness, however he may ruin the Beatrices of this world – Sammy is the character through whom Mr Golding, one suspects, is beginning to be reconciled to the loss of the primal Eden.

It has been suggested by an American scholar (and the irony of the labelling must appeal to Golding) that he does not write novels, but fables. There is some truth in this, but it is not the whole truth. Where most fables and allegories and satires fail is in their lack of individual reality. The idea is more important than the figure which gives it life. But Golding has never fallen into this trap. He is intensely, blindingly aware of physical immediacy. Whatever they may symbolise his schoolboys (for instance) exist as sharply differentiated individuals. Most important of all, he has an intimate, concrete, cosmic awareness of nature in the raw, and a poet's gift of words for describing it. His characters, as Professor Kermode memorably wrote,

live in a world of rock and sea and amoebae heaving in the pull of the moon, refusing to be locked fast by human imaginings of good or evil, obstinately talking its own language of sucking, plopping and roaring, against the human language which gives it another kind of life.

Though in *Free Fall*, with its re-affirmation of human spiritual potential, the symbolic emphasis has shifted to the microcosm, it remains true that his narrowing of focus in one sense is Golding's strength: it releases him into cosmic awareness. Despite all his self-imposed limitations, he remains the most powerful writer, the most original, the most profoundly imaginative, to have turned his hand to fiction in this country since the war; and if he never wrote another word his place in English letters would be secure.

SOURCE: essay in *Transactions and Proceedings of the Royal Society of Literature* XXXII (1963), pp. 37–57; based on a lecture given in 1960.

NOTES

[Reorganised and renumbered from the original – Ed.]
1. *London Magazine*, IV (May 1957), pp. 45–6. [Golding contributed to a symposium entitled 'The Writer in his Age' – Ed.]
2. Frank Kermode, *Spectator* (22 Aug. 1958), p. 257.
3. See Jacquetta Hawkes, *Man on Earth* (1954), pp. 98 ff.
4. W. J. Harvey, *Essays in Criticism*, VIII (1958), pp. 184–5.
5. Ian Gregor and Mark Kincaid-Weekes, *Twentieth Century*, CLXVII (1960), pp. 115–25.

Samuel Hynes (1976)   'Moral Models'

I am very serious. I believe that man suffers from an appalling ignorance of his own nature. I produce my own view, in the belief that it may be something like the truth. I am fully engaged to the human dilemma but see it as far more fundamental than a complex of taxes and astronomy.

William Golding wrote these words in reply to a literary magazine's questionnaire, 'The Writer in His Age'.[1] The questionnaire raised the question of 'engagement': should the writer concern himself with the political and social questions of his time? Golding's answer is unequivocal: the job of the writer is to show man his image *sub specie aeternitatis*. It is in this sense of engagement, not to the concerns of the moment but to what is basic in the human condition, and in the forms that this engagement has led Golding to create, that his uniqueness lies;

he is *the* novelist of our time for whom the novel matters because of what it can mean, and what it can do.

In the note from which I quoted above, Golding described himself as 'a citizen, a novelist and a schoolmaster'. The latter term is no longer literally applicable, but there is still a good deal of both the citizen and the schoolmaster in the novelist. The citizen is concerned with 'the defects of society'; the schoolmaster is concerned to correct them by proper instruction; the novelist finds the appropriate forms in which man's own nature may be embodied, that he may learn to know it. One consequence of this will-to-instruct is that Golding is an unusually disciplined, schematic writer; he thinks his novels out very slowly, and in careful detail (he wrote *Lord of the Flies*, he said, 'as if tracing over words already on the page'), and he is willing, even eager, to discuss what they mean. Another consequence is his desire to have his works read with the same kind of conscious intelligence, and his distrust of irrational and intuitive views of literary creation. He clearly thinks of his novels as the expressions of conscious intentions that existed before the writing began. Indeed he has twice spelled out what those intentions were. This does not, of course, imply that they took the form of abstract moral propositions which were then clothed in plot; but it does suggest that for Golding the entire plan of the work, *and* the meaning of that plan, were worked out first – that he started with meaning rather than with character or situation. Golding's own glosses of the meanings of *Lord of the Flies* and *Pincher Martin* have not seemed satisfactory to most readers – the teller in fact supports Lawrence's view of the creative process, and not Golding's; nevertheless, the fact that Golding thinks of his books as he does tells us something useful about the forms that they have taken.

There is no adequate critical term for that form. Golding himself has called his books both *myths* and *fables*, and both terms do point to a quality in the novels that it is necessary to recognise – that they are unusually tight, conceptualised, analogical expressions of moral ideas. Still, neither term is quite satisfactory, because both imply a degree of abstraction and an element of the legendary that Golding's novels simply do not have, and it seems better to be content with calling them simply *novels*, while recognising that they have certain formal properties that distinguish them from most current fiction.

The most striking of these properties is that Golding so patterns his narrative actions as to make them the images of ideas, that is to say, carries meaning apart from the meanings implied by character or those stated more or less didactically by the author. 'In all my books', Golding has said, 'I have suggested a shape in the universe that may, as it were, account for things.' To direct the attentions of his readers to that shape, Golding has chosen situations that isolate what is basic, and avoid both the merely topical and the subjective existence of the author. All but one of his novels [sc. those written up to the time of Hynes's study – Ed.] employ a situation that is remote in time or space, characters who are radically unlike the author, and a narrative tone that is removed, analytical and judicial. Consequently we must look for human relevance to the patterned action itself; if we 'identify', it must be with the moral – with the conception of man and the shape of the universe – and not with this character or that one.

The forms that Golding uses carry implications both for the kind of action selected and for the kind of characters involved in it. Since Golding proposes to embody general truths in his novels, he is committed, one would think, to select those human experiences that can be viewed as *exemplary*, not merely as *typical*; it is not enough to propose that a fictional event might happen. To be justifiable in a Golding novel an event must also bear its share of the patterned meaning. Consequently the novels tend on the whole to be short and densely textured, and the characters, while they are usually convincingly three-dimensional human beings, may also function as exemplars of facets of man's nature – of common sense, or greed, or will (one of Golding's most impressive gifts is his ability to make characters exemplify abstractions without *becoming* abstractions).

What we acknowledge if we choose to call Golding a fabulist is not that the total story is reducible to a moral proposition – this is obviously not true – but rather that he writes from clear and strong moral assumptions, and that those assumptions give form and direction to his fictions. But if Aesop and La

Fontaine wrote fables, we need another term for Golding. We might borrow one from scholastic aesthetics, and call them *tropological*, meaning by this that the novels individually 'suggest a shape in the universe', and are constructed as models of such moral shapes. Or if tropological seems too rarefied, *moral models* will do. The point, in any case, is to suggest the patterned quality of Golding's work, and to recognise the assumptions which that quality implies. Golding accepts certain traditional ideas about man and his place in the world: that mind, by meditation and speculation, may arrive at truth; that it may find in the past, meanings which are relevant to the present, and available through memory; that it may appropriately concern itself with metaphysics and with morals. Not all of these ideas are current now, certainly not in the avant-garde, and consequently Golding's work may seem, in the context of his time, more didactic and moralising than in fact it is. For though Golding is a moralist, he is not a moral-maker, and his novels belong, not with Aesop's fables, but with the important symbolic novels of our century – with Camus's and Kafka's. . . .

SOURCE: extract from 'William Golding', in George Stade (ed.), *Six Contemporary British Novelists* (New York, 1976), pp. 165–9 – revised version of an essay originally published in 1964 in the Columbia 'Essays on Modern Writers' series.

NOTES

1. [Ed.] *London Magazine*, IV (May 1957), pp. 45–6.

Norman Page Golding's Sources
(1985)

The 'sources' of a writer's art, potentially at any rate, include everything that has ever happened to him: every experience or thought, sensation or conversation, and not least every book he has read. In this essay I shall use the term in the much narrower sense of *literary* sources: those earlier texts that, whether good or bad, help in major or minor ways to shape a particular work of literature. Recently it has become fashionable to employ the term 'intertextuality' to refer to the fact that some books, rather than – or as well as – 'imitating' life (to use the time-honoured and question-begging terminology) or holding the mirror up to nature (as Hamlet puts it), are 'about' other books. This is actually no new discovery, and the scholars of past generations who examined Milton's debts to Homer and Virgil, or Fielding's to Cervantes and Lesage, recognised its importance. Parodies and translations are extreme instances of texts generated by other texts; but to a greater or lesser extent the phenomenon is widespread and certainly not confined to modern writers. If Eliot's *The Waste Land* is a patchwork or echo-chamber of other poems, so is Gray's *Elegy*.

The source in question does not need to be a major work of literature or even a very good one, and the relationship towards it of the work that (in part) derives from it is not necessarily admiring or respectful. This point is especially relevant to Golding. P. N. Furbank has noted that his novels 'tend to use some simple-minded literary ancestor as their starting-point', and suggests that the value for Golding of these second-rate and sometimes obscure works is that they give him something to which his own books can stand as counterblasts or rejoinders:

The earlier novels, with their simple and false ideology, provide a jumping-off point, inviting him to turn them upside down in the light of his own special vision of original sin. Jack, Ralph and Piggy emphatically do *not* put on a 'good show' like Ballantyne's Jack, Ralph and Peterkin Gay; and Golding's Pincher Martin, unlike his predecessor, is a very unwilling hero.[1]

This is, of course, rather like the way in which parody works, by offering a superficially similar but fundamentally different version of the original in order to expose its limitations. Golding's purpose, however, goes far beyond the local and limited one of parody. For him, what I am referring to as the 'source' is like a speech in a debate with which he takes passionate and ironic issue, seeming to exclaim or murmur, 'But life – or human nature – isn't like that. . .'.

Often he makes no secret of his sources: *Coral Island* is explicitly referred to on the last page of *Lord of the Flies*, and the epigraph of *The Inheritors* is a quotation from H. G. Wells's *Outline of History*. He is particularly fond of allusive titles – *Lord of the Flies* and *Darkness Visible*, for instance – that challenge the reader to identify, and then to consider the relevance of, their origins. At other times the parallels may be less openly acknowledged, and may even have been unconscious. But the term 'parallels', in spite of its air of geometrical precision, is a vague one and comprehends both isolated allusions and the kind of relationship, positive or negative, that permeates an entire book. In the comments on individual novels that follow, examples of all of these levels of influence will be encountered. Whatever terminology we use, however – 'debts', 'borrowings', 'parallels', 'influences', or 'sources' – it is important to recognise that what Golding is doing is to make a *creative* use of a great variety of sources. He does not take it for granted that our admiration for the original, and our pleasure in being reminded of it, will gain him a bonus, as Matthew Arnold does when he imitates the classical epic simile in 'Sohrab and Rustum'; nor is the spotting of the source indispensable to a grasping of the writer's point, as it is in Jane Austen's satire on the Gothic novel in *Northanger Abbey*, or Byron's send-up of Southey in *The Vision of Judgment*.

Lord of the Flies quickly announces itself as belonging to that sub-genre of science fiction which looks into the future and is perhaps most widely associated with H. G. Wells. But a more significant relationship is to R. M. Ballantyne's juvenile novel *Coral Island* (1857), the centenary of which was just around the corner when Golding's own novel appeared. Ballantyne's story tells of three boys – Ralph, Jack and Peterkin – who, finding themselves on a tropical island, proceed to build a society in a spirit of cheerful co-operation and imperturbable goodwill. Golding retains the first two names, but substitutes for Peterkin (which would sound implausible to contemporary ears) that of Simon, presumably recalling the disciple and saint who was 'Simon called Peter'.

Golding himself has declared that 'one book never comes out of another, and *The Coral Island* is not *Lord of the Flies*. . . . one work does not come from another unless it is still-born'.[2] What one makes of this depends on what meaning is to be attached to 'comes out of' and 'come from'. If these phrases imply mere imitation, of the kind to be found (for example) in attempts by neo-classical poets to emulate 'the ancients', or attempts by nineteenth-century poets to write Shakespearean verse-drama, it is true that the results are usually lifeless. But there are abundant instances of major works that have 'come out of' others: *Samson Agonistes* and *The Family Reunion* come out of Greek tragedy, as *Ulysses* comes out of Homer and *The Pilgrim's Progress* out of the Bible. What seems crucial is whether the later work has a life of its own, or (as with a popular writer trying to capitalise on a success by means of a sequel) is *simply* an imitation.

This is where Golding's habit of using an earlier work critically, contrastively, and even parodically, in novels that have been described as 'reactive experiments',[3] comes in. Obviously '*The Coral Island* is not *Lord of the Flies*', and if it were there would have been no need to write the latter. But *Lord of the Flies* is what it is, and not otherwise, partly because of its relationship to the Victorian boys' book. Rather as Eliot in *The Waste Land* briefly evokes the 'Sweet Thames' of Elizabethan London as an economical way of making a point about modern squalor and disillusion, Golding allows Ballantyne's optimistic tale of survival and self-discipline to stand for a whole set of beliefs and attitudes that he sets about contradicting and demolishing. It may be objected that there is some over-simplification involved in taking a single book to represent the values and outlook of a whole civilisation, and the objection is not groundless. The year 1857, after all, saw the publication not

only of *Coral Island* but of *Little Dorrit*, Dickens's most
pessimistic novel. However, for better or worse, this boldly
contrastive, even schematic, method is of the essence of
Golding's art. Just as parodists are not always scrupulously fair
to their victims, Golding's dialectical technique derives some of
its force from an intolerance of the other man's point of view.

Although Golding's attitude to Ballantyne's novel seems
somewhat patronising[4] (see, for example, the ironic reference
to it on the last page of *Lord of the Flies*), it served his purpose;
and he seems to have intended the reader to take into account
the way in which one book uses the other. For example, as well
as using some of Ballantyne's names he gives us more than one
explicit allusion, most strikingly on the final page ('Like the
Coral Island'), with its irony that is the more telling for being
unconscious on the speaker's part. And to read Ballantyne after
reading Golding is to be made aware of numerous proleptic
ironies: for instance, Peterkin Gay's description of the island as
'the ancient Paradise' reminds us that Paradise was not only
beautiful and fertile but the setting for the Fall.

Several other novels have been identified as parallels to, if
not influences upon, *Lord of the Flies*. *The Swiss Family Robinson*
(1813), by the Swiss author Johann Rudolf Wyss, is another
juvenile story widely read in earlier generations and offering
the same kind of comfortable optimism as Ballantyne's book.
But any story of survival on a tropical island inevitably recalls
one of the earliest of English novels, Defoe's *Robinson Crusoe*
(1719). Again, any relationship between Defoe's and Golding's
novels must be seen as contrastive or 'reactive', since Crusoe's
thirty-year preservation of his reason and piety is a far cry from
the rapid moral deterioration of the modern schoolboys. (Four
years after *Lord of the Flies*, Muriel Spark published *Robinson*,
which makes more explicit use of Defoe's novel.) When *Lord of
the Flies* appeared, several reviewers compared it with Richard
Hughes's *A High Wind in Jamaica* (1929), which also presents the
fate of children left to their own devices as a result of
catastrophe. But Golding has stated that he did not read
Hughes's book until after he had written his novel, so that the
relationship between them can be no more than an interesting
parallel. Finally, and more problematic, is the question of

Conrad's *Heart of Darkness* (1899), to which the phrase 'the darkness of man's heart' a few lines from the end of *Lord of the Flies* appears to be an allusion. Writing at the very end of the Victorian age, Conrad expresses in this, one of the earliest modernist texts, a pessimism that is much closer to Golding than to Ballantyne; and it is tempting to follow up the resemblance by suggesting that the pig's head in Golding's novel may owe something to those decapitated heads on stakes that Conrad's Marlow finds when he reached Kurtz's settlement in the heart of Africa. Again, however, the source-hunter's enthusiasm is checked by Golding's statement in an interview that he had 'never read' Conrad's story.[5] It might be maintained that he would not need to have read it to know the title, of which his own phrase quoted above is a paraphrase; but it looks as though any substantial debt is out of the question.

Lord of the Flies looks to the not-too-distant future, *The Inheritors* to the remote past. Its starting-point seems to have been H. G. Wells's *Outline of History* (1920). The epigraph of *The Inheritors* offers Wells's view of Neanderthal man: 'gorilla-like', 'repulsive', the likely origin of the ogre in folklore. The same view is dramatised in Wells's story 'The Grisly Folk', published in 1921 and included in collections of his short stories. This deals with the first encounters between Neanderthals and *Homo sapiens*, and must also be seen as a source for Golding's novel. Again, however, the influence works by contraries. Golding uses Wells in the second novel, as he had used Ballantyne in his first, as a point of departure, a convenient (because simplistic and easily demolished) representative of a set of views – optimistic, confident, progressivist – that his fiction tries to expose as hollow. Wells, the heir of Darwin, views evolution as a process of improvement, a development from lower to higher states in the moral as well as the intellectual and physical spheres; Golding questions this whole assumption, since the New Men who drive out the innocent Neanderthals are capable of evil. As J. S. Ryan has said, the title seems to allude ironically to the Gospels, 'since it is not the meek who inherit the earth but the killers of the meek'.[6] (The title *The Inheritors* had, incidentally, been used in 1901 for a novel on which Joseph Conrad and Ford Madox Hueffer had collaborated, but the resemblance seems to extend no further.)

Pincher Martin looks neither to the future nor to the remote past. It appears to be a novel of the present day or the immediate past, and evidently draws on the author's own wartime experiences, but it actually turns out to refer to the timeless state of existence after death. A number of sources and parallels have been proposed. The most striking of them is an all-but-forgotten book with virtually the same title: *Pincher Martin, O.D. A Story of the Inner Life of the Royal Navy* (1916), by Commander Taprell Dorling, a once widely-read author who used the pseudonym 'Taffrail'. Golding seems to have read the book at one time but has denied owing anything to it but the title. Unconscious memory may have played a part, however, since J. S. Ryan, who has made a careful comparison of the two novels, suggests that 'the dependence of the one on the other is considerable . . . almost every person and action in the Golding novel can be found to have a parallel or antithesis in the earlier novel'.[7] It is also tempting to see the phrase 'Inner Life' in Taffrail's subtitle as being taken up, and taken more seriously, by Golding.

To a lesser extent, the story 'An Occurrence at Owl Creek Bridge' (1891) by the American author Ambrose Bierce is worth considering. This ingenious and effective short story owes its power to a final twist or gimmick – the same abrupt concluding reversal that Golding has so often been praised or blamed for. The hero, whose escape and return home has been narrated, is found to have died at an early stage of the story. Other sources that have been suggested are Wells's story 'The Remarkable Case of Davidson's Eyes' (1895), which has some striking elements in common with *Pincher Martin* (which also uses the name Davidson); *Coral Island* (again), which includes an episode in which a pair of seaboots are washed ashore; and a poem 'Rockall' by Michael Roberts, first published in 1939 and included in Roberts's *Collected Poems* (1958), which contains the lines:

> The waves break on the bare rock; the traveller remembers
> Shipwreck, the struggle with the waters, the wild climb . . .

That Golding had Rockall in mind as the apparent site of Martin's ordeal (not that the Atlantic offers much competition) is confirmed by a punning reference to it in the novel.[8]

Free Fall, Golding's fourth novel but the first in which he essays something closer to the traditional realistic mode of fiction, has obvious affinities with the *Bildungsroman* (novel of growth and development) and *Künstlerroman* (novel about the artist) of which such works as Joyce's *Portrait of the Artist as a Young Man* and Lawrence's *Sons and Lovers* are familiar examples. It does not, however, make use of earlier books so obviously or so importantly as the fables that preceded it, though the title has suggested one significant comparison to several critics, who have seen it as echoing that of a very recent book, Albert Camus's *The Fall* (original title, *La Chute*: 1956). The similarities between the two have been discussed at length by Bernard S. Oldsey and Stanley Weintraub, who also suggest that the episode in Sammy's cell may owe something both to Edgar Allan Poe's story 'The Pit and the Pendulum' and to George Orwell's *1984*.[9]

Some other suggestions may be briefly noted. Peter Green has called *Pincher Martin* 'Aeschylean' (see his essay, above), recognising the similarity of situation between Golding's protagonist and that of Aesychlus's *Prometheus Bound*. The relationship is again a 'reactive' one, since whereas Aeschylus's hero is persuaded to submission, Golding's, like that of Shelley's *Prometheus Unbound*, refuses to submit. Gabriel Josipovici has suggested that *Robinson Crusoe* must also be seen as a shadowy presence behind Golding's novel, and has stressed the way in which the latter is a logical sequel to *The Inheritors*. Golding's intention in *Pincher Martin* is 'to isolate one of the new men, the "inheritors", and thus to explore what man is like – not what he thinks he is like, but what, stripped of the protective clothing of civilisation, he really is'.[10] The notion of isolation readily brings to mind Defoe's archetypal hero; and just as in *The Inheritors* Golding had used Wells's *Outline of History*, so in its successor (Josipovici argues) he 'takes yet another classic of rational liberalism'. Once more, the novelist's attitude towards the earlier book is sceptical and ironic: although Martin tries to 'tame' the rock and reduce its starkness to a semblance of the civilised world, as Crusoe does with his much more hospitable and amenable island, his attempt is doomed to failure, as Crusoe's is not.

The Spire is a historical novel in which, paradoxically, Golding seems to have dispensed with sources. Although one might have expected the author of a story set in the Middle Ages, and dealing with the construction of a readily identifiable building, to have gone to contemporary documents or later historians, Golding insists that he did nothing of the sort. In an interview with Jack I. Biles, he states that he 'didn't do any research for this book', but had long lived near Salisbury Cathedral and worked in its shadow, and had a general interest in churches and a keen awareness of the 'technology' that went into their building. Hence he had no need to go to books: the understanding was in his bones, and *The Spire* was 'easy to write'.[11] It appears that an earlier title was *Barchester Spire*, and the book was actually advertised under that title in 1961. (On its echoes of Trollope, see David Skilton's essay in Part Three, below.)

In an interesting essay, D. W. Crompton has drawn attention to some other fruitful sources for *The Spire*.[12] Browning's poem 'The Bishop Orders his Tomb at Saint Praxed's Church' (1845) includes an Anselm who has much in common with the Anselm of Golding's novel; moreover, 'the theme of Browning's poem obviously has some relevance to the relationship between Jocelin and his aunt, the Lady Alison'. More importantly, the Norse myth of Balder, revived by more than one Victorian poet, 'is . . . essential to the construction of *The Spire*'. Most important of all, according to Crompton, is Ibsen's play *The Master Builder* (1892), in which the protagonist has formerly been a builder of churches and has been in the habit of ascending the spires he has sent up into the sky – a symbolic expression of his ambition and pride. Yet another source has been referred to by P. N. Furbank: the novel *The Nebuly Coat* (1903) by J. Meade Falkner, which is 'overshadowed . . . by a tottering minster tower'.[13]

In an interview given in America in 1962, after Golding had disclosed that he had read neither *Heart of Darkness* nor *A High*

Wind in Jamaica before writing *Lord of the Flies*, the interviewer asked him, with a touch of desperation, how he felt about 'the parallels between the two works'. Golding replied:

> There is a parallel, I think, but like so many literary parallels it's the plain fact that if people engage in writing about humanity, they're likely in certain circumstances to see something of the same thing.[14]

This is obviously good sense, but some of the examples given earlier in this essay suggest that something considerably more than a 'parallel' is at times involved. The question inevitably arises whether we can expect an author always to be fully aware of the works that in one way or another have influenced him. Again, common sense suggests that the influence may sometimes be unconscious; but this is a view that Golding has dogmatically rejected. When another interviewer quoted D. H. Lawrence's dictum 'Never trust the teller, trust the tale', he replied:

> Oh, that's absolute nonsense. But *of course* the man who tells the tale if he has a tale worth telling will know exactly what he is about and this business of the artist as a sort of starry-eyed inspired creature, dancing along, with his feet two or three feet above the surface of the earth, not really knowing what sort of prints he's leaving behind him, is nothing like the truth.[15]

In spite of this, a good deal of evidence suggests that a significant part of the creative process is not conscious. Dickens, for example, was startled at the unconscious self-revelation when it was pointed out to him that he had given his hero David Copperfield his own initials reversed.

Golding has always taken an infectious pleasure in poking gentle fun at the earnest enquiries of academics, including source-hunters. The following exchange comes from a recent interview:

> INTERVIEWER: Were you influenced . . . by the theories of J. J. Bachofen in his *Myth, Religion and Mother Right?*
> GOLDING: Never heard of him. What was he?[16]

There is conceivably some slight affectation in his protestations of ignorance, for he is a well-read man with a wide-ranging and eclectic tastes. Still, it seems to be true that his novels are not 'researched' in any systematic way: he writes about the things he knows and understands, and sometimes that knowledge and understanding have been nourished by his reading. Of the decision to set his historical novel *Rites of Passage* (1980) in the Regency period, he has remarked casually: 'I happened to have a great deal of source material in my head.'[17]

There remains one important literary influence, general and pervasive rather than specific and localised: that of the drama, especially Greek tragedy and Shakespeare. In the same interview, Golding states:

> I was more or less brought up on Shakespeare and that has an influence. . . . there's no doubt that I know my Shakespeare pretty well by heart. . . . I don't think my novels come out novels. If they owe anything to previous work, and obviously they must, it's the theatre much more than novel writing. It's great drama in particular. I think of the shape of a novel, when I do think of a novel as having a shape, as having a shape precisely like Greek drama.[18]

These are far-reaching influences, and operate on more than one level. If the 'shape' of Greek tragedy helps to determine the structure of a Golding novel and to account, for example, for his fondness for such devices as 'discovery' (*anagnorisis*) and 'reversal' (*peripeteia*), the language of Shakespeare's plays must be seen as influencing the extraordinarily rich, dense and complex prose of Golding's novels.

SOURCE: specially written for, and first published in, this Casebook.

NOTES

1. P. N. Furbank, 'Golding's Spire' (review of *The Spire*), *Encounter*, XXII (May 1964), p. 59.

2. Bernard F. Dick, 'The Novelist is a Displaced Person'; An Interview with William Golding', *College English*, XXVI (1965), p. 481.

3. Bernard S. Oldsey and Stanley Weintraub, *The Art of William Golding* (New York, 1965), p. 36.

4. He has, however, defended two other juvenile island-stories – *The Swiss Family Robinson* and *Treasure island* – in his essay, 'Islands', *Spectator*, 204 (10 June 1960), pp. 844–5; repr. in *The Hot Gates* (1965).

5. James Keating, 'Interview with William Golding', in James R. Baker and Arthur P. Ziegler, Jnr (eds), *William Goldings's 'Lord of the Flies'* (New York, 1964), p. 194.

6. J. S. Ryan, 'The Two Pincher Martins: From Survival Adventure to Golding's Myth of Dying', *English Studies*, LV (1974), p. 142.

7. Ibid., pp. 144, 146.

8. Bierce's story and Roberts's poem are suggested as sources or parallels by Peter Green in his essay 'The World of William Golding' (excerpted in Part Two, above), pp. 49–50.

9. Oldsey and Weintraub, op. cit., p. 116.

10. Gabriel Josipovici, *The World and the Book* (London, 2nd edn, 1979), p. 243.

11. Jack I. Biles, *Talk: Conversations with William Golding* (New York, 1970), pp. 96–7.

12. D. W. Crompton, '*The Spire*', *Critical Quarterly*, IX (Spring 1967), p. 66.

13. Furbank, op. cit.

14. Keating, op. cit., pp. 194–5.

15. Frank Kermode, 'The Meaning of it All', *Books and Bookmen* (Oct. 1959), p. 9.

16. James R. Baker, 'An Interview with William Golding', *Twentieth Century Literature*, XXVIII (1982), p. 139.

17. Ibid., p. 161.

18. Ibid., pp. 131–2, 165. For a comparison between *Lord of the Flies* and the *Bacchae* of Euripides, see Bernard F. Dick, *William Golding* (New York: Twayne, 1967), pp. 29–33.

PART THREE

Studies on Individual Novels

C. B. Cox   On *Lord of the Flies* (1960)

William Golding's *Lord of the Flies*, published in 1953, is a retelling in realistic terms of R. M. Ballantyne's *The Coral Island*. A group of boys, shot down during some kind of atomic war, are marooned on an island in the Pacific. In contrast to the boys in Ballantyne's story, who after a number of exciting adventures remember their time on the island as an idyllic interlude, the children in *Lord of the Flies* soon begin to quarrel, and their attempts to create an ordered, just society break down. On one level the story shows how intelligence (Piggy) and common sense (Ralph) will always be overthrown in society by sadism (Roger) and the lure of totalitarianism (Jack). On another, the growth of savagery in the boys demonstrates the power of original sin. Simon, the Christ figure, who tries to tell the children that their fears of a dead parachutist are illusory, is killed in a terrifying tribal dance. The Lord of the Flies is the head of a pig, which Jack puts up on a stick to placate an illusory Beast. As Simon understands, the only dangerous beast, the true Lord of the Flies, is inside the children themselves. Lord of the Flies is the Old Testament name for Beelzebub.

Lord of the Flies is probably the most important novel to be published in this country in the 1950s. A story so explicitly symbolic as this might easily become fanciful and contrived, but Golding has mastered the art of writing a twentieth-century allegory. In contrast to the medieval audience, the general reading public today does not believe that correspondences exist between the material and spiritual world, and they do not automatically expect every incident or object to have symbolic importance. No conventions of allegory exist, and the writer cannot introduce colours, animals, flowers or any of the other emblems which were available for the medieval writer. In these circumstances, many novelists have given objects an arbitrary symbolic meaning. In Iris Murdoch's *The Bell*, for example, there is no inherent reason why the bell under the lake should represent absolute values, and so her fanciful developments of plot to illustrate this meaning often appear rather forced. This type of allegory can fully succeed only if the literal sense is dramatically coherent in its own right, as in Camus's *The Plague*. There are other methods of writing twentieth-century allegory, of course, as in Kafka's use of fanciful situations to explore psychological and religious experiences; but if a story based on real life is used, then there must be no unlikely situations or fanciful embroidery. A modern audience will accept the underlying meanings only if they are conveyed in a completely convincing, true to life series of events.

To find an exciting, stimulating plot which is both dramatically credible and capable of allegorical interpretation is exceptionally difficult. The idea of placing boys alone on an island, and letting them work out archetypal patterns of human society, is a brilliant technical device, with a simple coherence which is easily understood by a modern audience. Its success is due in part to the quality of Golding's Christianity. He is neither puritan nor transcendentalist, and his religious faith is based upon his interpretation of experience, rather than upon an unquestioning acceptance of revelation. Although his four novels [sc. those written up to the time of Cox's essay – Ed.] deal with the depravity of man, he cares deeply about the condition of human life, and shows great compassion for men who suffer and men who sin. His religious sense does not make him turn from life in disgust, but proves to him the dignity and importance of human action. In development of plot, descriptions of island and sea, and treatment of character, he explores actual life to prove dramatically the authenticity of his religious viewpoint.

Lord of the Flies is a gripping story which will appeal to generations of readers. It is easy to despise the power of a good story, and to think of moral implications as an alternative to the obvious devices of surprise, suspense and climax. But to succeed, a good story needs more than sudden deaths, a terrifying chase and an unexpected conclusion. *Lord of the Flies* includes all these ingredients, but their exceptional force derives from Golding's faith that every detail of human life has a religious significance. This is one reason why he is unique among new writers in the '50s, and why he excels in narrative ability. Typical of the writers of the '50s is an uncertainty about human values, a fundamental doubt about whether life has any importance whatsoever. In contrast, Golding can describe friendship, guilt, pain and horror with a full sense of how deeply meaningful these can be for the individual. The terrible fire which kills the young children, the fear of Ralph as he is pursued across the island, and Piggy's fall to his death on the rocks make us feel, in their vivid detail, Golding's intense conviction that every particular of human life has a profound importance. His children are not juvenile delinquents, but human beings realising for themselves the beauty and horror of life.

This faith in the importance of our experiences in this world is reflected in Golding's vivid, imaginative style. He has a fresh, delightful response to the mystery of Nature, with its weird beauty and fantastic variety. The conch, which Ralph and Piggy discover in the lagoon and use to call the children to assemblies, is not just a symbol of order. From the beginning Golding does justice to the strange attraction of the shell, with its delicate, embossed pattern, and deep harsh note which echoes back from the pink granite of the mountain. When towards the end of the story the conch is smashed, we feel that sadness which comes when any object of exquisite beauty is broken. The symbolic meaning, that this is the end of the beauty of justice and order, is not forced upon us, but is reflected through our emotional reaction to the object itself.

In this way Golding expresses his passionate interest in both physical and moral life. His narrative style has an unusual lucidity and vitality because he never forgets the concrete in his search for symbolic action:

Now a great wind blew the rain sideways, cascading the water from the forest trees. On the mountain-top the parachute filled and moved; the figure slid, rose to its feet, spun, swayed down through a vastness of wet air and trod with ungainly feet the tops of the high trees; falling, still falling, it sank towards the beach and the boys rushed screaming into the darkness. The parachute took the figure forward, furrowing the lagoon, and bumped it over the reef and out to sea.

With admirable simplicity this passage conveys a multitude of effects. The incident is part of an exciting story, a surprising climax to the murder of Simon; at the same time the dead parachutist is the 'beast' to the children, a symbol of adult evil, which, by their own act of killing, they have shown to be part of themselves. But the passage achieves its strong emotional impact because it is so firmly grounded in physical awareness. Water cascades from the forest trees, the parachutist 'furrows' the lagoon. These precise words describe with physical immediacy a situation which is real and dramatically poignant. And the picture of the man treading the tops of the high trees recalls the mystery of human life, with its incredible inventions, and yet also makes us feel deep compassion for the ungainly feet, the horror of death.

The island itself is boat-shaped, and the children typify all mankind on their journey through life. In the opening scenes the island has the glamour of a new-found paradise. With the green shadows from the palms and the forest sliding over his skin, Ralph is overcome by wonder. He lolls in the warm water, looking at the mirages which wrestle with the brilliance of the lagoon. But soon the terrifying fire transforms the island, and illusion gives way to reality. In nightmares the children begin to be afraid that this is not a good island; they become accustomed to the mirages, 'and ignored them, just as they ignored the miraculous, throbbing stars'. The beauty of the earthly paradise grows stale to their eyes. At the end they leave behind them 'the burning wreckage of the island', whose loveliness has been degraded by their presence.

As his attempts to discipline the boys begin to appear hopeless, Ralph, on a search for the illusory beast, sees beyond the lagoon out to open sea:

The lagoon had protected them from the Pacific: and for some reason only Jack had gone right down to the water on the other side. Now he saw the landsman's view of the swell and it seemed like the breathing of some stupendous creature. Slowly the waters sank among the rocks, revealing pink tables of granite, strange growths of coral, polyp, and weed. Down, down, the waters went, whispering like the wind among the heads of the forest. There was one flat rock there, spread like a table, and the waters sucking down on the four weedy sides made them seem like cliffs. Then the sleeping leviathan breathed out – the waters rose, the weed streamed, and the water boiled over the table rock with a roar. There was no sense of the passage of waves; only this minute-long fall and rise and fall.

This creature becomes a part of Ralph's consciousness, a symbol of a reality he tries to avoid. As he watches the ceaseless, bulging passage of the deep sea waves, the remoteness and infiniteness of the ocean force themselves upon his attention. By the quiet lagoon he can dream of rescue, but the brute obtuseness of the ocean tells him he is helpless. It is significant that the two boys who are killed, Simon and Piggy, are taken back to this infinite ocean.

As the waves creep towards the body of Simon beneath the moonlight, the brilliantly realistic description of the advancing tide typifies all the beauty of the world which promises eternal reward to those who suffer:

Along the shoreward edge of the shallows the advancing clearness was full of strange, moonbeam-bodied creatures with fiery eyes. Here and there a larger pebble clung to its own air and was covered with a coat of pearls. The tide swelled in over the rain-pitted sand and smoothed everything with a layer of silver. Now it touched the first of the stains that seeped from the broken body and the creatures made a moving patch of light as they gathered at the edge. The water rose further and dressed Simon's coarse hair with brightness. The line of his cheek silvered and the turn of his shoulder became sculptured marble. The strange, attendant creatures, with their fiery eyes and trailing vapours, busied themselves round his head. The body lifted a fraction of an inch from the sand and a bubble of air escaped from the mouth with a wet plop. Then it turned gently in the water.

Here we become aware of the Christian meaning underlying the story. For Ralph the sea typifies the insensitivity of the universe, but this is to see it from only one point of view. The multitudinous beauties of the tide promise that creation was not an accident; after our suffering and confusions are over, a healing power of great beauty will solve all problems. The advancing waves are like moon-beam-bodied creatures, gently washing the body of Simon free from all stain, and dressing him in pearls, silver and marble in token of the richness of his love for the other children. Instead of seeking to introduce ancient myths into the modern world, Golding creates his own, basing his symbols on the actual wonder of life itself. The intricate beauty of the waves is not merely a pleasing arrangement of light and matter, but an incredible manifestation of the wonder of creation, with a valid life in our consciousness. As Simon's body moves out to open sea under the delicate yet firm lifting of the tide, it seems impossible that his sacrifice has had no ultimate meaning.

The island, the sea and the sacrifice of Simon all show Ralph the truth of the human situation. His mind finds the burden of responsibility too great, and he begins to lose his power to think coherently: 'He found himself understanding the wearisomeness of this life, where every path was an improvisation and a considerable part of one's waking life was spent watching one's feet.' Jack's return to savagery, taking all the children with him, is portrayed with frightening realism. The lust for killing grows too strong, and Ralph's inadequate democratic machinery cannot keep it in check. Behind their painted faces, the children can feel a security, a lack of personal responsibility for the evil they perpetrate, and this desire explains the growth of Jack's prestige. When he tells them they will not dream so much, 'they agreed passionately out of the depths of their tormented private lives', and he is amazed by their response. Only the intelligence of Piggy is not tempted by the tribal dances, and his character is presented with great compassion. His fat, asthmatic body is a natural butt for children, and continual mockery has taught him to be humble and to enjoy being noticed even only as a joke. But he has a powerful belief in the importance of civilised order, and gradually Ralph learns to appreciate his value. His death is a poignant reminder of the unjust and cruel treatment given by society to so many good men.

Simon is perhaps the one weakness in the book. We see his friendship for Ralph, when he touches his hand as they explore the island, and his love of all people when he ministers to the dead body of the parachutist, but alone among the characters his actions at times appear to be motivated, not by the dramatic action, but by the symbolic implications of the story. At the beginning, when he withdraws at night from the other children, his motives are left uncertain. But the scene where he confronts the lord of the flies is most convincing. In this pig's head covered with flies, he sees 'the infinite cynicism of adult life'. He has the courage to face the power of evil, and, knowing that the beast is in all of them, he climbs the hill to find out the truth about the dead parachutist.

The whole story moves towards Simon's view of reality. The growth of savagery forces Ralph to make strange speculations about the meaning of human identity. When they hold an assembly at nightfall, he is surprised at the different effect made by the darkness:

Again he fell into that strange mood of speculation that was so foreign to him. If faces were different when lit from above or below – what was a face? What was anything?

He faces the possibility that there is no absolute perspective to human life, and that all experience may be meaningless. He longs to return to the world of adults, and the irony of this illusion is shown when, after a battle in the skies, the dead parachutist comes down 'as a sign from the world of grown-ups'. At certain stages of the story, Golding deliberately makes us forget that these are only young children. Their drama and conflict typify the inevitable overthrow of all attempts to impose a permanent civilisation on the instincts of man. The surprising twist of events at the end of the novel is a highly original device to force upon us a new viewpoint. The crazy, sadistic chase to kill Ralph is suddenly revealed to be the work of a semi-circle of little boys, their bodies streaked with coloured clay. But the irony is also directed at the naval officer, who comes to rescue them. His trim cruiser, the sub-machine gun, his white drill, epaulettes, revolver and row of gilt buttons, are only more sophisticated substitutes for the war-paint and sticks of Jack and his followers. He too is chasing men in order to kill, and the dirty children mock the absurd civilised attempt to hide the power of evil. And so when Ralph weeps for the end of innocence, the darkness of man's heart, and the death of his true, wise friend, Piggy, he weeps for all the human race.

Source: essay in *Critical Quarterly*, ii (1960), pp. 112–17.

Mark Kinkead-Weekes & Ian Gregor 'Approaches to *The Inheritors*' (1967)

To come to *The Inheritors* fresh from *Lord of the Flies* is to be made quickly aware of opacity and puzzle not present in the earlier novel. We feel uncertain about both the direction of the narrative and the status of the characters, and it is often difficult to see, on the simplest level, what exactly is going on. It is only as we continue to read that we begin to place our difficulty. The style is simple enough, with a vivid sensuousness that carries us forward in spite of uncertainties. The difficulty lies in the point of view:

> As he watched, one of the farther rocks began to change shape. At one side a small bump elongated then disappeared quickly. The top of the rock swelled, the hump fined off at the base and elongated again then halved its height. Then it was gone.

It is because we are placed behind a pair of eyes that only perceive, and cannot understand, that we may have no more idea than Lok what it is that he is watching. Perception is itself, no more; not what we normally expect it to be, a stepping stone to an idea rapidly transferred from the eye to the mind. We come to realise that Golding's Neanderthalers live through their senses. They can infer to a limited extent from their own experience but they cannot go beyond it because they cannot deduce or reason. What we watch is the moment when Neanderthal Man first confronts Homo Sapiens, but all we can be given is sharply focused visual detail of shape and movement. Lok cannot conceive a human creature with a nature wholly unlike his own; cannot deduce such a creature from the behaviour he sees; and consequently cannot understand that behaviour at all. We share his limitations as we use his eyes.

It is of course open to us to use our own reasoning powers on his experience. At several points before this one we could have deduced not only the existence of New Men but the difference in nature between them and Lok's People. They must have removed the communal bridge-log to make their own huge fire; it was their smoke that caused Lok to make his almost fatal mistake on the cliff; they must have been responsible for the disappearance of Ha. As we watch the instinctive miming of Lok the tracker we can accurately deduce the differing natures of Men and People, and hazard a shrewd guess at what must have happened to Ha; and once we have deduced Man's hostility, suspicion and fear, the opacity vanishes and Lok's vision sharpens for us. What he watches so uncomprehendingly is a Man treating him as though he were a predatory enemy, a man not 'another', as simple loving and fearless as himself, but peering stealthily round and above the rock he uses as cover, spying.

Any such process of understanding has, however, to take place outside the fiction itself. The only incitement to interpret, deduce, explain, comes from our own intellectual frustration at being confronted with the apparently unintelligible. This is not what concerns Golding. The response he seeks is essentially the imaginative one of knowing what it is like to look through eyes empty of thought and as innocent of judgement as of hatred, suspicion and fear. He had devoted all his resources to creating that experience, and Lok's incomprehension is a vital part of it. We cannot be prevented from analysing and judging, nor need we; but we would indeed 'murder to dissect' if we thought that analysis and judgement were supposed to be the object of the exercise. Imaginative exploration, through a vision quite unlike our own, comes first. Understanding will follow, but more slowly and mysteriously from a distillation of experience and it may result in something far more complex than a black-and-white contrast between Men and People. If ever there was a book meant to be read through in one imaginative act, by which we seek to become, and to judge only when the experience is complete, it is *The Inheritors*.

Any account of the novel that does not centre on its qualities of imaginative exploration ought then to be highly suspect. It is easy to suggest apparently useful ways of looking at it, but it is more important to see just how they miss the mark. The epigraph suggests, for example, that Golding wishes to overturn H. G. Wells's account of the Neanderthaler (both in *The Outline of History* and his tale *The Grisly Folk*) as *Lord of the Flies* had subverted Ballantyne. So one could approach the novel as a fictional essay in prehistory, based on considerable knowledge of anthropology, and seeking to substitute a truer picture of Neanderthal Man for one distorted by faulty assumptions. The funeral of Mal, for instance, comes across vividly in just this archaeological and anthropological way.

Yet the novel is also a fictional *tour de force*, taking us to an otherworld and othertime that we enjoy for their own sake, irrespective of historical considerations. Isn't this science fiction if it is science at all: taking us backwards as space fiction takes us forwards, substituting Neanderthalers for Martians, but giving us the same pleasure in the exotic, or the familiar seen through strange eyes?

Yet again, the fiction seems to point to allegory. Golding's Neanderthalers are the true innocents, the harmless ones, not only without evil themselves but incapable of understanding it when it meets and destroys them. They run to meet their killers in love, and are quite incapable of preserving themselves by destroying their oppressors. The title reveals a bitter irony, for it is not the meek who inherit the earth but the killers of the meek. We can contrast every aspect of the 'fallen' life of the New Men with the 'unfallen' life of the People, and take home to ourselves the message that comes from realising the nature of our ancestry. We may then reach the point when the novel seems no longer essentially about Neanderthal Man at all, but merely uses him as a way of analysing the nature of the Fall. Emblems now emerge: the dead tree from which Lok and Fa look down on the destruction of their Eden; the waterfall which marks the limit of innocence, but beyond which the sinful have to travel towards a line of darkness.

Each of these ways of looking seems momentarily convincing; each indeed contains an aspect of truth; but as soon as one turns back to the novel itself, all are manifestly unsatisfactory, suggesting something smaller and less valuable than what is actually there. For what they all leave out of account is the primary experience of reading: a reaching out through the imagination into the unknown. The mode of *The Inheritors* is one of discovery, not an exercise in literary archaeology, science fiction or a fable about the Fall. By committing himself so radically to the viewpoint of his People, by doing his utmost to ensure that he is kept out of his normal consciousness, Golding does contrive to see things new, not merely see new things. His imagination is at full stretch throughout because of the challenge of his basic form; it has to be, for the novel to be written at all. That is the real significance of the point of view.

SOURCE: extract from *William Golding: A Critical Study* (London, 1967), pp. 67–70.

Samuel Hynes (1976)   On *Pincher Martin*

. . . Both formally and intellectually, *Pincher Martin* is the most impressive of Golding's novels. It is also the most difficult, because its form is an involved representation of time and consciousness, and because what it has to say about death is heterodox and complex. It bears certain family resemblances to the two preceding novels: it uses the literature of survival in much the same way that *Lord of the Flies* uses island literature, and it treats an unusual condition of consciousness, as *The Inheritors* does. Like the earlier two, it is a novel with a moral 'program', which deals schematically with the problem of evil and its consequences.

But it is also different from the others in important ways. The primary difference is that the form of *Pincher Martin* does not compel a moral interpretation from the beginning; rather it offers first a vivid survival-adventure, and then reverses itself, and says: What you have been taking as objectively true is in fact false – or true in another paradoxical sense. This is an uncommon fictional technique, but by no means a unique one; satires like *Gulliver's Travels* play tricks with our expectations, and so do the symbolic tales of Poe and Kafka. The difference in Golding's technique is that he goes to considerable trouble to make the apparent seem particularly real *before* he allows the symbolic quality of the action to appear overtly. As a result the grounds of reality shift within the novel, and the reader's relation to the action is unstable and ambiguous; this in turn compels a more attentive reading (or rereading) of the book – the symbolic meaning is more difficult to grasp because it appears in the final chapters as a *new* interpretation of data which we have already interpreted in a conventional, realistic way.

The action of the novel thus divides into two parts, with a coda. The first part takes Christopher Martin from the moment when a torpedo blows him off the bridge of his destroyer through the events of his efforts to survive on a barren rock. In these ten chapters Golding creates, in sharp, circumstantial detail, the conditions in which Martin's extraordinary will-to-survive operates. The sea, the rock, the creatures that live on it, the weather – all are meticulously set down. So, too, is Pincher Martin, fiercely acting out his ego; and the vividness with which Golding has drawn this figure is in itself a remarkable achievement, since we do not see Pincher's personality reflected from any other human being, but only in relation to hostile nature, and to itself.

This lonely survivor we must regard as admirable, simply because he clings to life so tenaciously, and against such odds (how can we *not* side with Man, against Nature?). His endurance, his will, his ingenuity are all heroic – he is a man opposing adversity, refusing to be annihilated. And when he cries 'I am Prometheus', we see what he means – he is a man trapped on a barren rock, defying the fate that put him there.

But woven into this heroic narrative are flashbacks of Martin's past that establish a character who is the opposite of heroic – an unscrupulous egoist who has stopped at no depravity, no betrayal of love and friendship, to nourish his own ego. By seeing *this* character developed parallel to the

Promethean survivor, we are forced to acknowledge that the same qualities that have kept him alive against such odds are the qualities that make him morally repulsive. And so in the middle of the eleventh chapter we face a moral dilemma: on what grounds can we condemn those qualities by which man survives?

The answer comes in the following three chapters, beginning with the moment when Martin looks down into the sea from his rock, and sees a *red* lobster, and realises that perhaps his whole effort to survive – rock and all – has been a subjective creation, an act of the will asserting itself against necessity. He has invented it all, ingeniously, but not perfectly; he has forgotten that only boiled lobsters are red, and that guano is insoluble, and he has arranged the rocks on which he survives like the teeth in his own mouth. From this point on, the apparent reality of Pincher's survival begins to dissolve, and with it his own surviving personality, until at the end he is reduced to two hands, red and grasping like lobster claws, and symbolic, as his nickname is symbolic of his essential nature. And then even these claws are worn away, and Pincher Martin as a personality is annihilated.

But what does it all mean? The coda is there to give us some clues. In the last chapter, as in the final chapter of *The Inheritors*, Golding provides a new perspective, a shift in point of view out and away from the agent of the action, by which we can regard the action more deliberately and objectively. We are on an island in the Hebrides when a naval party lands to pick up the body of a drowned sailor (Pincher Martin). An islander, called Campbell, is moved and disturbed by the experience, and asks the officer in charge of the party, 'Would you say there was any – surviving? Or is that all?' The officer, like the one at the end of *Lord of the Flies*, misunderstands the question, and replies: 'If you're worried about Martin – whether he suffered or not. . . . Then don't worry about him. You saw the body. He didn't even have time to kick off his sea-boots.'

If Pincher didn't have time to kick off his seaboots, then the moment in the first chapter when he apparently *did* kick them off was illusory, and if that was illusory, then so was everything that came after, and we must go back and reinterpret what we have read. Survival in *Pincher Martin* is survival in the ordinary sea-story sense after all: Golding has used the 'man-against-the-sea' conventions here just as he used the desert island conventions in *Lord of the Flies*, to provide a system of expectations against which to construct a personal and different version of the shape of things.

Some readers have felt cheated by this last-sentence reversal of their assumptions about the nature of reality in the novel. But in fact Golding has placed a number of clues to Pincher's state earlier in the novel, and the sea-boots should come as the clincher; the clues are scattered and concealed, like the clues in a mystery novel, in order that the reader should discover the truth late in the book, and with surprise, but they are there. This device of discovery is dramatic, but it is more than that; it is a way of making an important point about the meaning of death. Though Martin dies on page two, this physical death is passed over: there are kinds of dying that are more important than that instant of merely physiological change. (Golding's American publisher made this point clearer by calling the novel *The Two Deaths of Christopher Martin*.) An audience for which Campbell's question about eternity was a vital one would surely have no trouble in understanding the paradoxes of living-into-death and dying-into-life that inform the novel; it is only to rational materialists (for whom Pincher is a type) that a novel about varieties of dying will seem an outrageous violation of reality.

Pincher Martin is so tightly and intricately interwoven as to read like a difficult poem; one must attend to its symbols and images in order to understand its narrative action, and indeed there is little that one could call *plot* in the book. The sequence of events is determined, not by the interaction of character and environment as in conventional novels, but by the necessities of the symbolic form in which Golding has expressed his theme. So many readers found this form difficult that when the novel was dramatised on the BBC Third Programme, Golding provided his own account of the theme:

Christopher Hadley Martin had no belief in anything but the importance of his own life; no love, no God. Because he was created in the image of God he had a freedom of choice which he used to centre the world on himself. He did not believe in purgatory and therefore when he died it was not presented to him in overtly theological terms. The greed for life which had been the mainspring of his nature, forced him to refuse the selfless act of dying. He continued to exist separately in a world composed of his own murderous nature. His drowned body lies rolling in the Atlantic but the ravenous ego invents a rock for him to endure on. It is the memory of an aching tooth. Ostensibly and rationally he is a survivor from a torpedoed destroyer: but deep down he knows the truth. He is not fighting for bodily survival but for his continuing identity in face of what will smash it and sweep it away – the black lightning, the compassion of God. For Christopher, the Christ-bearer, has become Pincher Martin who is little but greed. Just to be Pincher is purgatory; to be Pincher for eternity is hell.

We must, of course, he cautious about accepting an artist's own version of his work; in Golding's case, the novels tend to expand and live beyond his programs. Nevertheless, this account gives a lead into the novel. We may start with the question of what it is to be Pincher.

It is, first of all, simply to be a man called Martin in the Royal Navy; 'Pincher' is a nickname habitually attached to sea-going Martins, just as in the American services all Mullinses are called 'Moon'. But Pincher *is* a pincher – his Deady Sin is Greed, and he eats everything he touches. Pincher is a devourer of life, 'born with his mouth and his flies open and both hands out to grab'. The grabbing hands, which are imaged in the novel as lobsters, are the last part of Pincher to disappear at the end.

This supreme greed is expressed in the novel in a parable, the Parable of the Chinese Box. One of Pincher's victims describes how the Chinese, when they wish to prepare a rare dish, bury a fish in a tin box. Maggots eat the fish, and then one another, until finally 'where there was a fish there is now one huge, successful maggot. Rare dish'. Pincher is the huge successful maggot, devouring the other maggots and crying, 'I'll live if I have to eat everything else in this bloody box!'

Pincher's greed, however, is not a motive in itself; it is the means by which he preserves the only value in his world – his own personality. Those human attributes that assert identity – speech, thought, the consciousness of consciousness – are his goods; and loss of identity – as in sleep and ultimately death – is his evil. In his past life he has used other people to reassure himself on his own existence, as he has used photographs and mirrors. But on the rock there are no mirrors, and his identity-card photograph is blurred, and there is no one to touch; his existence there is therefore one fierce effort to preserve his personality, to assert that, 'I am what I always was', and later simply 'I am! I am!' Pincher, in his efforts to assert that because he thinks, he is, is simply the modern heir of Descartes: man proving his own existence from the inside out. Starting with mind, he creates his own world in which all meaning and value is in *self*; and all outside self is meaningless mechanism, the material upon which mind plays, and on which self feeds.

This egocentric version of reality not only relates Pincher to the Cartesian tradition; it also connects with his 'I am Prometheus'. Prometheus is *the* mythic hero of humanistic, liberal man: he is the man-befriender, the God-defier, the indestructible life-worshiping identity whose own existence gives meaning to his suffering, and whose suffering affirms his existence. One might expect that Golding, the disillusioned ex-liberal, would consider Prometheus a symbol of that conception of man which he finds most immoral; and *Pincher Martin* might well be subtitled 'The Case Against Prometheus'. Golding establishes this point by making Pincher's Promethean heroism simply one more case of his self-creating egoism; Pincher *plays* Prometheus (he is, after all, a professional actor), to appropriate imaginary background music by Tchaikovsky, Wagner and Holst: 'it was not really necessary to crawl', Golding observes, 'but the background music underlined the heroism of a slow, undefeated advance against odds'. This is not heroism, but a parody of it; and indeed *parody* describes pretty well the overall relationship between what Pincher imagines himself doing and the reality – he is a parody Robinson Crusoe, a parody Hamlet, a parody Lear, a parody Lucifer. But he is one reality – Pincher, the clutching claws.

Strictly speaking, there is no character in the novel except Pincher; his isolation is complete from beginning to end. The naval officer and Campbell in the last chapter have no particular definition, and even the persons who people Pincher's memories and visions are not really characters, because Pincher has regarded them not as separate human beings but as things to be devoured. One figure, however, stands in an important symbolic relation to Pincher; the existence of his friend Nathaniel is interwoven with Pincher's in the way that good is interwoven with evil, dark with light. Nathaniel is a religious man and something of a mystic; he lectures on 'the technique of dying into heaven', and he warns Pincher to prepare for death. Like his biblical namesake he is a man 'in whom is no guile'; no doubt we are also meant to recall Christ's words to Nathaniel: 'Hereafter ye shall see heaven open, and the angels of God ascending and descending upon the Son of man.' Nathaniel is the opposite of Pincher; he can love selflessly and without thought, and he therefore wins the love of Mary, the girl for whom Pincher feels an obsessive lust.

The most important single scene in the novel is probably the one in which Nathaniel explains his eschatology to an amused Pincher. Man must learn, says Nathaniel, the technique of dying into heaven, in order to make himself ready for heaven when death comes. 'Takes us as we are now and heaven would be sheer negation', he says. 'Without form and void. You see? A sort of black lightning, destroying everything that we call life . . .' If we do not prepare ourselves for heaven (*heaven* here meaning simply eternity described spatially), then we will die into the sort of after life that our natures invent. This, it is clear, is what has happened to Pincher; the rock is the heaven he has invented for himself, a barren rock like a tooth, without life except of the lowest sort, a place in which the only possible value is bare survival. Pincher's heaven is the appropriate fate of a man who has lived as he has lived; but because it is his own invention, it is not eternal. It exists by an act of will, and when his will fails, and he admits that he cannot believe in the objective existence of his invention, then the black lightning comes and annihilates him.

The final incident of Pincher's existence is a visionary interview with a mysterious figure in seaman's clothes, who is God. 'What do you believe in?' God asks. 'The thread of my life', Pincher replies. 'I have created you and I can create my own heaven.' 'You *have* created it', says God. And in God's presence the world of rock and sea stops moving, becomes painted paper, cracks, and drops into 'absolute nothingness'.

Pincher Martin is an eschatological novel, a myth of dying; nevertheless, it is more concerned with life than with death (perhaps this is true of all such works), and Golding uses the ambiguities of time and reality in Pincher's survival narrative to make moral points about man's attitudes toward death as they affect his attitudes toward life. From the right view of the selfless act of dying, the right moral principles will follow; Nathaniel is a somewhat obscure embodiment of those principles, Pincher of their negation. The central point of the novel seems to be simply this: death is the end of identity. If we accept this, we will prepare for the end of identity, and will value what is personal and individual in our existence less (as saints have always done), and we will fear death less because the loss of identity will be familiar and acceptable to us. Whether indeed we will live in a 'heaven' of our own invention if we die unprepared is of no importance, except as a symbolic way of representing the terrors of death to an identity-preserver, a Pincher.

When Golding was asked about the 'mythical aspect' of Pincher, he replied that Pincher was 'a fallen man . . . Very much fallen – he's fallen more than most. In fact, I went out of my way to damn Pincher as much as I could by making him the most unpleasant, the nastiest type I could think of, and I was very interested to see how critics all over the place said, "Well, yes, we are like that". I was really rather pleased.' He should not have been surprised that responsive readers found in this 'nastiest type' an image of their natures. Like all of Golding's major characters Pincher is an embodiment of a proposition about human nature, rather than an individual; in so far as we recognise greed as a sin to which we are prone, we *must* say, 'Yes, we are like that'.

But this generalised quality in the central figure is also the principal limitation of the novel. Pincher is not a credible, individualised character as we understand character in most fiction; he exists in conditions that strip him of personality – indeed that is the symbolic point of the action – and leave him simply *a* human creature. The rock is the most real thing in the book, and Pincher is most real in his survivor-relation to it;

when we see him in flashbacks with other persons he becomes a stock melodramatic villain, the Handsome Seducer. The symbolic action engages us – and engages us with more force than either *Lord of the Flies* or *The Inheritors* does – because it is barer, more entirely symbolic. But it does so at the expense of other expectations that are part of our general feeling for fiction – that there shall be persons with whom we can ally ourselves existing in a believable world, that we shall experience life being lived. *Pincher Martin* is an extraordinary achievement, a moral document that is also a work of art, in which moral meaning is entirely embodied in artistic form. But its excellence is also its limitation, and it is not an excellence that could be repeated. . . .

SOURCE: extract from 'William Golding', in George Stade (ed.), *Six Contemporary British Novelists* (New York, 1976), pp. 188–98 – revised version of an essay originally published in 1964 in the Columbia 'Essays on Modern Writers' series.

Sylvère Monod   Golding's View of the Human Condition in *Free Fall* (1982)

. . . It is tempting to see Golding's earlier fiction in two main blocks, with *Free Fall* as a kind of belated appendage to the original three novels, followed by the looser pair of *The Spire* and *The Pyramid* (linked by the striking similarity of their titles, if by nothing else).

If *Free Fall* (1960) is in the nature of an appendage to William Golding's first three published novels, it is nevertheless markedly different from them. It has something in common, undoubtedly, with *Pincher Martin*, in that both novels concern themselves with the retrospective glance cast by a man over his past life and particularly over his misdeeds. But even with *Pincher Martin* the differences are much more striking than the similarities; *Free Fall* has none of the sensational purgatorial gimmickry used in the earlier novel to explore Christopher Martin's psychology and morality. The least insular of Golding's novels so far, *Free Fall* is in many ways a new departure in the author's career.[1]

Curiously enough, the position of *Free Fall* in William Golding's own liking and estimation seems to be consistently low. I find that I am by no means the only person, or the only Frenchman, to whom the novelist has said as much (in the course of a private conversation held in May 1976), quite unambiguously. It is of course readily understandable that Golding should have a special fondness for *Lord of the Flies* which made him famous. As for the rest, perhaps *Free Fall* is in fact too different from those other children of his brain to have endeared itself to him. If it was, as suggested above, a new departure, the author may feel that it took him into a dead end. However that may be, William Golding has not expressed himself about *Free Fall* as he has done about *Lord of the Flies*, a state of things which, as will appear later, is not without its advantages.[2] In default of the author's own comments, however, let us consider a few representative opinions. The originality of the novel is generally recognised. Oldsey and Weintraub see it as 'unique in Golding's work'.[3] Kinkead-Weekes and Gregor call it 'the most elusive and difficult of Golding's novels'.[4] And Henri A. Talon, who clearly resents or deplores *Free Fall* on the whole, defines that novel as 'of his works the one most fraught with experience'.[5] Talon goes on to add, with lavish use of inverted commas, that *Free Fall*, rather than 'a "true" novel', is 'a "montage" of situations' (p. 66). Oldsey and Weintraub are less reserved in their admiration: 'Golding's ability to hold, balance and juggle scenes so that eventually they come down in place is extraordinary . . . it has gone . . . probably high enough to be fairly compared with Camus's classic structure'.[6] And Mark Kinkead-Weekes and Ian Gregor write, yet more reassuringly, that 'it is surely not perverse to claim the book as a considerable achievement'.[7]

Reassuringly to me, for that is precisely the claim I wish to make for *Free Fall*.

A vivid liking and admiration for *Free Fall* (or even, as in my case, a preference for *Free Fall* over the author's other works of fiction) may seem to imply a lack of appreciation for the other Golding, or Goldings. One cannot speak of the *ordinary* Golding, for he is never ordinary and never made it a habit to write one specific kind of fiction, but one may speak of the *real* Golding and there is reason to believe that he would accept such a definition of himself as the author of *Lord of the Flies*, *The Inheritors* and *Pincher Martin*; a preference for *Free Fall* thus boils down to a preference for the *realist* Golding over the real Golding, or creator of fables, allegories and myths.[8] Not that there is no myth in *Free Fall*.[9] Not that the early trio had contained no realistic elements or had not been concerned, like *Free Fall*, with the human predicament. But they had expressed that preoccupation less straightforwardly.

The major question about *Free Fall*, considering Golding's constant ambition and also taking into account his specific aim, the question by the answer to which the novel stands or falls, may well be: what does Golding tell his reader through that novel about mankind and mankind's fate that is true, important and, if not entirely new, at least worth hearing?

Oldsey and Weintraub in their detailed comparison between *Free Fall* and Albert Camus's *La Chute*,[10] have convincingly shown that the two works have more in common than their names. The central theme of Golding's novel – if not all his fiction – brings to mind another great French work of our time, André Malraux's *La Condition humaine* (the human predicament).

The two words of Golding's title are significant in themselves as well as through their association, they possess 'both theological and scientific connotations'.[11] The theological, or at any rate moral, aspect probably predominates over the scientific, which serves only as a metaphor. But the very real and acute problems faced by the narrator, Sammy Mountjoy, are those of freedom (and/or free choice, free will) and of the Fall, the fall of man, the fall of Everyman, regarded as ineluctable and inborn. Sammy repeatedly asks himself the same question or questions: when did he lose or alienate his freedom, when did he fall from his childhood state of grace? The loss of freedom and the fall of man are one and the same event, which Sammy Mountjoy (predestined by his ironical name, it would seem, to descend into sorrow rather than mount in joy) finds it very hard to pinpoint, however hard he tries. As the loss of freedom and the fall result from a man's use of his free will, the whole problem is one of guilt and responsibility. Mark Kinkead-Weekes and Ian Gregor's masterly chapter on *Free Fall* is based on Golding's essential concern 'with *Being*, not *Becoming*'.[12] But, even through their careful analysis and discussion, it appears that Being and Becoming cannot be wholly separated. 'What I was', Sammy claims, 'I had become' (p. 100).[13]

A complementary aspect of the human predicament also examined in *Free Fall*, and on which Golding lays great stress, is the lack of stability and even permanence in the human personality. That view is not new of course, Oscar Wilde had been much struck by the impossibility of identifying oneself (i.e., one's present self) with the remembered image of oneself (i.e., one's past self) acting, feeling or writing, some time ago – not even necessarily very long ago. In his essay 'Pen, Pencil and Poison', Wilde wrote: 'The permanence of personality is a very subtle metaphysical problem, and certainly the English law solves the question in an extremely rough-and-ready manner.'[14] Closer to us, two remarkable though unaccountably neglected novels by Rayner Heppenstall, *The Connecting Door* and *The Woodshed*, both published in 1962 and thus of later date than *Free Fall*, explored the same psychological and moral difficulty. The *Connecting Door*, in particular, goes one better by staging in a spectacular and graphic manner the confrontation between three of a man's successive selves. I do not wish to go into details here, having already done so elsewhere.[15] But I would like to point out that this perception of an important phenomenon belonging to the condition of man, of modern man at any rate, forms part of the value, interest and modernity of Golding's *Free Fall*. The author has not invented a device comparable to Heppenstall's in *The Connecting Door* (where

Harold Atha, in the course of his third visit to a city in the East of France, meets, and holds converse with, both Harold and Atha, i.e., with the persons he had been on the occasion of his two earlier stays in the same city). But his procedure for placing Sammy Mountjoy face to face with several of his earlier selves is nonetheless original and effective.

How is it done? In great part through narrative technique, and more precisely, through the manipulation of time. Without going into details of plot, we note that an obvious characteristic of *Free Fall* is the absence of chronological sequence in the narrative. But there is a deliberate purpose behind the shuffling of the sections. In the first three, Sammy Mountjoy looks back, fairly consecutively (but not quite) at his childhood; in sections 4, 5 and 6, his story has taken a great leap forward to the period when he has become an art student, lives in London, seeks out his former schoolfellow Beatrice Ifor, courts her, forces her to become his very unsatisfactory mistress, and finally deserts her as soon as he has fallen in love with another woman whom he marries. Section 7 takes another jump ahead to a time when Sammy is a prisoner-of-war in a German camp, being questioned by one Dr Halde, who attempts in vain to make him denounce the prisoners planning to escape; because of his refusal to answer Dr Halde's questions, Sammy is locked up in a dark room. The scheme becomes slightly more complicated at this stage, for in section 8, before the two following sections relate his harrowing experiences in the dark cell, Sammy reminisces; it is not quite clear whether he does so in the cell itself (in which case we should have him in the book, as so often, reminiscing about reminiscing) or by recalling the experiences in the cell at some later period, beyond the point reached by the narrative by the end of the book, at the time when he is conducting his searching self-examination. Section 8 begins with the query 'How did I come to be so frightened of the dark?' (p. 117). The answer to that question enables him to bridge a great part of the gap left between sections 3 and 4, explaining in passing that, although originally the pauper orphaned son of a decayed prostitute, he had been adopted by Watts-Watt, a kindly but tormented and ridiculous clergyman, and thus enabled to go to art school. Sections 9–10, then, deal with the experiences in the dark cell. Sections 11 and 12 make up another extended flashback and complete the stop-gap narrative begun in 8 (of the period of Sammy's adolescence and schooldays, originally left unfilled-in between 3 and 4). Section 13 has to do with a much later, i.e., more recent, post-war, time, when Sammy visits Beatrice Ifor in a mental hospital where she carries on her incurably wrecked existence. There remains only a very brief fourteenth section reverting to the end of the dark cell episode and disclosing one essential fact about it, i.e., that the terrors of the cell (in fact an ordinary cupboard) had been made up solely by Sammy's own imagination and sick fears.

So that the real, historical chronology of Sammy's *Bildungsroman* rests on the following sequence of the sections in the book: 1, 2, 3, 8, 11, 12, 4, 5, 6 (here, a still unbridged time-gap), 7, 9, 10, 14, 13. The number of these sections calls only for brief comment. Unlike *Lord of the Flies*, which has just twelve (like *The Inheritors* and *The Spire*, while *Pincher Martin* runs to fourteen, twelve being reputedly the most harmonious or classical figure), *Free Fall* is thus composed of thirteen units and a coda (or *cauda*), the units being of uneven length and irregularly organised.[16] Whether or not Golding chose the figure thirteen deliberately, it so happens that thirteen as a number is small, odd, prime, supposedly unlucky (or, through inverted superstition, lucky), and in every way adapted to this story and study of Sammy Mountjoy, the bastard, the eccentric, the artist, the odd man out in so many ways.

The technique of shuffling the time-units may well be regarded as owing something to such predecessors of William Golding as Joseph Conrad and the founding father of flexibility in the novel, Laurence Sterne. The technique has some traditional weight and significance. In fact, the resulting time-pattern is both psychologically and morally convincing: psychologically, because as far as we know, the human mind is much less methodical than any form of printed narrative; memory never yields a continuously chronological sequence of events (that is a significant distinction between memories and memoirs, or – in French – between *une mémoire* and *un mémoire*); it jumps back and forth, juxtaposes and conflates episodes, etc. Morally, the quest for guilt and responsibility is much assisted by the potentialities of such a time-pattern: Sammy can thus short-circuit many impeccable chains of explanations, and embrace at one glance the consequence and the cause, however remote from each other in time, and conversely he can send his mental searchlight at will further and further back into his past. To say that the time-pattern in *Free Fall* is convincing is not to say that it is life-like; it is of course arbitrary and contrived (like all organised narrative); but it makes the book readable as well as meaningful, and it enables the narrator to be constantly confronting and comparing segments of his past, as though his life were given back to him on index-cards instead of in a bound volume or on an unbroken recorded tape. 'Time', Sammy writes, 'is two moods. The one is an effortless perception native to us as water to the mackerel. The other is a memory, a sense of shuffle fold and coil, of that day nearer because it is more important, of that event mirroring this, or those three set apart, exceptional and out of the straight line altogether' (pp. 5–6). Mountjoy thereby gains the possibility of conducting his search more profoundly, of investigating really meaningful relationships between persons or incidents, of producing what Talon finely called 'the superficially sinuous yet profoundly coherent evocation of the past'.[17] A straightforward chronological narrative can perhaps achieve similar results, though at a greater cost, and with less of the fruitful freedom that a book called *Free Fall* demands and deserves.

The method is not everything. The method is only, after all, the medium, and the medium is not *all* the message, though there would be no message without a medium to convey it. In spite of the current unpopularity of the notion that art must, or even that art may, have a message, that a work of art may be, or may include, a statement, I find it extremely difficult to discuss Golding in other terms, or, for that matter, to believe that he would have greatly cared to write *Free Fall* if he had not wished to say something, to convey ideas to his readers. No doubt that is what he means when he says: 'I have been trying to write the sort of thing I would define as "significance literature" '; or when he refers to 'the novel which tries to look at life anew'.[18] Let us therefore review such general statements as *Free Fall* contains, and attempt to define their overall significance.

I suppose many readers will have been mildly irritated by the opening pages of *Free Fall* which are almost entirely made up of general statements, many of them sufficiently portentous: 'Free-will cannot be debated but only experienced' (p. 5, in fact the very first page of the novel). 'We are dumb and blind yet we must see and speak . . . To communicate is our passion and our despair' (p. 7). They are interspersed with Sammy Mountjoy's self-questionings (as a man) and posturings (as narrator) in a way reminiscent of the tricks and manners of the garrulous Victorians, even including an address to the reader, though not, of course, to the dear, or the gentle, reader. 'Then why am I writing this down?' (p. 6) 'To communicate . . . With whom then? You? . . . No. Not with you . . . And who are you any way? Are you on the inside, have you a proof-copy? Am I a job to do? Do I exasperate you by translating incoherence into incoherence?' (p. 7). Golding's or Sammy's reader is thus treated as someone clearly neither dear nor gentle, someone to be met with a mixture of arrogance and cunning. It would be a pity to let oneself be irritated, to the point of being deterred, by the slightly pretentious note in this beginning. Every reading after the first one will provide evidence that the opening section has its uses, that the archness and slackness belong to Sammy and indeed characterise him thus early.[19] Besides, every word counts, it will be discovered on returning to that section, or on remembering it, and contributes in striking the keynote and heralding the treatment of the major themes.

Among the general statements in the later portions of *Free Fall* we find: 'Man is not an instantaneous creature . . . He is an incredible bundle of miscellaneous memories of feelings, of fossils and coral growths' (p. 36); 'No man can tell the whole truth' (p. 140); 'Perhaps consciousness and the guilt which is unhappiness go together' (p. 60); 'Only the things you cannot avoid, the sear of sex or pain, avoidance of the one suffering repetition and prolongation of the other, this constitutes what your daily consciousness would not admit, but experiences as life' (p. 110); 'What men believe is a function of what they are; and what they are is in part what has happened to them' (p. 161); 'Useless to say that a man is a whole continent, pointless to say that each consciousness is a whole world because each consciousness is a dozen worlds' (p. 189). Such phrases and questionings add up to a valid, coherent view of life, profoundly pessimistic in tone. Sammy Mountjoy is not a pleasure to contemplate, least of all to himself. He may be a great artist, but he is a sorry specimen of humanity, although at the same time a representative specimen, being very much (apart from his artistic gift) the *homme moyen sensuel*, trapped in the shackles and limitations of the human predicament.[20] Golding seems to have intended his reader to become conscious, to *gain* awareness, of his (or her) kinship with Sammy. There are Mountjoy-like trends and impulses in all human beings because such trends and impulses, unpalatable as they are, are part of human nature. But for this awareness to be a gain, and not a dead loss of hope, we must step beyond the desolating perception.

Sammy is bound to accept responsibility for some misdeeds, or for acts of his which involved enduring unhappiness for others. But he repeatedly finds that he could not have acted otherwise than he did, being what he was: 'I had lost my power to choose. I had given away my freedom . . . What I was, I had become' (p. 100). Probably part of Sammy Mountjoy's theorising amounts to special pleading. It is comfortable or at least comforting for him to think that what men are is in part what has happened to them. He deceives himself, is a 'self-swindler', as Dickens put it in *Great Expectations* (ch. 28). But again Sammy is not unlike other human beings in this respect. All his elaborate effort to see, to understand, to communicate with himself, is adulterated by unconscious insincerity and by moral blindness.

The general conclusion, to put it simply, appears to be that evil and unhappiness are unavoidable, that it is man's fate both to inflict and to endure suffering. Evil and pain are everywhere. As all readers of *Lord of the Flies* know, 'the Beast is in us'. And presumably readers of *Lord of the Flies* realise that the *deus ex machina* in the guise of a naval officer will not always come to rescue us from ourselves; or if he comes it may be only to take us back into the uncertainties and potential horrors of nuclear warfare.

From William Golding's *Free Fall* there are two ways of

deriving encouragement. One seems to me mistaken. I admire and envy the readers who find moral support in their view of Sammy as redeemed by his ordeal in the dark cell and as emerging from it victorious in the end. B. S. Oldsey and S. Weintraub, for instance, claim that Sammy 'emerges from the cell with some portion of victory'; they believe that in the cell he 'has finally made use of man's last resource, prayer'. But it takes great ingenuity to perceive this, and more to demonstrate it. M. Kinkead-Weekes and I. Gregor, who comment in detail on the final section, do not reach the same conclusion. H. A. Talon, however, also believed that Sammy's cry in the dark cell – 'Help me!' (p. 140) – is the sign of his conversion.[21] In a way one wishes such readers were right, but I fear the ultimate significance of *Free Fall* is as bleak, as devoid of any explicit expression of hope as the view of mankind and mankind's fate at the core of *Lord of the Flies*, *The Inheritors* and *Pincher Martin*.

Is Golding then an out-and-out pessimist? He has contrived to make contradictory pronouncements on this very issue: 'I am by nature an optimist; but a defective logic – or a logic which I sometimes hope desperately is defective – makes a pessimist of me.'[22] Fortunately he has said nothing specifically about *Free Fall*, unless, as Kinkead-Weekes and Gregor contended,[23] the last line of the book ('The Herr Doktor does not know about peoples', p. 192) is a statement about hero and author as well, a view which I find attractive rather than convincing. William Golding has all too often been impish in his statements about his own writings.[24] But he has always been intransigently honest in his fiction. Let us trust the tale, rather than the teller.

The saving grace of Sammy Mountjoy and of the world depicted in *Free Fall* lies in the potential for compassion and communication. Lucid perception is saddening, because mankind offers at best a sorry sight; you may respond with Lady Macbeth: 'A foolish thought, to say a sorry sight', but William Golding apparently believes that it would be a more foolish thought *not* to say a sorry sight, and most foolish of all to content oneself with the saddening perception. Clear-sightedness is better than illusion; but it is not enough.

The writer's duty may be to denounce weaknesses and

frailties and perils. But he must at the same time lead his readers to realise that beyond his denunciation there may lie something else. Denunciation in itself would be meaningless and useless (or worse than useless, for it might act as an inducement to commit suicide), if it did not carry with it some positive possibilities, which need not necessarily be formulated by the writer. But his very act of denunciation cannot be accomplished in a moral or spiritual vacuum; preaching for nihilism is self-defeating. At any rate Golding does not espouse the Schopenhauerian form of pessimism echoed by George Gissing,[25] or by Thomas Hardy; his most pessimistic hope does not reside in an expectation that mankind will cease to desire life and its continuation and thus become peacefully extinct. William Golding's view comes closer to George Eliot's 'meliorism'; what he has created is a darker version of meliorism, tailored to suit the disillusioned, predominantly gloomy mood of our own century. In the face of evil in man and doom in the world, little can be done, but that little must be done. Mankind is of little value and cannot reasonably entertain or inspire very exalted hopes, but through sympathy, compassion, communication, solidarity, sharing, men and women can alleviate one another's sufferings. We may remember at this point that Sammy Mountjoy wrote: 'To communicate is our passion and our despair' (p. 7) and also that, after he has seen Beatrice Ifor in her decrepit state, he is genuinely moved: 'Suddenly the image of thick Beatrice started up behind my eyes, green, tense and nittering. I covered them with my hand' (p. 188). To me, there (rather than in the self-centred and cowardly fears experienced in Dr Halde's cupboard) lies the one redeeming moment. Realising the unhappiness of one other human being, realising that it has come to that other being through one's own act, is the most agonising experience imaginable. Shedding tears over that experience is, however fleetingly, cathartic. It enables Sammy to make contact with Kenneth, whom he hates and whose own motives are impure and selfish. I do not believe that Sammy ever prays, but at that point he feels.

Golding seems to be telling us that an honest mind which is not foolish or simplistic, unless it pins its faith and hope on

another life in another world, has very little to build on in its
struggle against utter pessimism. Dim is the solitary light that
shines over the bleak landscape of the modern world. Yet it is
enough to save man from utter hopelessness and to impart
meaning and purpose to artistic creation. And after all what do
we find in Golding's greatest predecessor in English literature,
in Shakespeare himself, if not a view of man as endlessly,
ineradicably disappointing, but at the same time perennially
and infinitely pathetic?[26]

SOURCE: essay in Douglas Jefferson & Graham Martin (eds),
The Uses of Fiction (Milton Keynes, 1982), pp. 250–60.

NOTES

1. See Mark Kinkead-Weekes & Ian Gregor, *William Golding: A Critical
Study* (London, 1967). While noting the link with *Pincher Martin* (pp. 161,
165), they consider that in *Free Fall* Golding for the first time abandoned the
'isolated and isolating settings' (p. 165) hitherto familiar to him.

2. He did, however, introduce one gimmicky reference (with a quotation)
to *Free Fall* in 'Tolstoy's Mountain' – see *The Hot Gates and Other Occasional
Pieces* (London, 1965), p. 123 – as the work of 'a contemporary'.

3. Bernard S. Oldsey & Stanley Weintraub, *The Art of William Golding* (New
York, 1965), p. 11.

4. Kinkead-Weekes and Gregor, p. 165.

5. Henri A. Talon, *Le Mal dans l'oeuvre de William Golding* (Paris, 1966),
p. 65. Talon's resentment is connected mainly with the hero's persistence in
making love to his impotent mistress (see pp. 76–7).

6. Oldsey & Weintraub, p. 122.

7. Kinkead-Weekes & Gregor, p. 198.

8. Although the best 'realistic' episodes in *Free Fall*, i.e., the early sections
about Sammy's childhood, comprise a powerful element of creative
imagination; at any rate they could hardly be more different from Golding's
own childhood, as described in 'Billy the Kid' (see *The Hot Gates*, pp. 159–65).

9. As is recognised by Kinkead-Weekes & Gregor and also, with
reservations, by Talon, who finds their analysis 'too subtle' (Talon, p. 66).

10. See Oldsey & Weintraub, ch. 5: 'Double Vision: *Free Fall* and *The Fall*'.

11. Oldsey & Weintraub, p. 105. Talon calls *Free Fall* by a French title of
his own coinage: *Liberté de la chute*.

12. Kinkead-Weekes & Gregor, p. 157.

13. All quotations from *Free Fall* are taken from the Penguin edition
(Harmondsworth, 1963, reprinted 1964). Section and page numbers are
given parenthetically in the text.

14. See *Essays by Oscar Wilde*, edited by Hesketh Pearson (London: 1950), p. 94.

15. See my 'Rayner Heppenstall and the *Nouveau Roman*', in Maynard Mack & Ian Gregor (eds), *Imagined Worlds* (London, 1968), pp. 461–75.

16. In at least *Lord of the Flies* the ideal figure is not achieved without artifice or deliberation, for the twelfth section would have lent itself to subdivision between its two disparate parts.

17. Talon, p. 78.

18. 'On the Crest of the Wave', *The Hot Gates*, pp. 126, 132.

19. Albert J. Guerard, in the 'Note on Method' prefixed to his book *The Triumph of the Novel* (New York, 1976), rightly insists on the essential difference between our first reading of any novel, and all later readings of the same.

20. As is fully recognised, e.g., by Samuel Hynes, who writes that Sammy is 'an ordinary, unheroic man, who insists on his representativeness': *William Golding* (New York, 1964), p. 33. And Golding himself has explained that in the 1950s he 'believed then, that man was sick – not exceptional man, but average man. I believed that the condition of man was to be a morally diseased creation' ('Fable', *The Hot Gates*, p. 87).

21. See Oldsey & Weintraub, pp. 118–19; Kinkead-Weekes & Gregor, pp. 194–9: Talon, p. 70.

22. In 'On the Crest of the Wave', *The Hot Gates*, p. 126.

23. Kinkead-Weekes & Gregory, p. 198.

24. As when he says that *Lord of the Flies* is a 'highly and diversely explicable book' (*The Hot Gates*, 'Fable', p. 98). Or, 'I regard myself as a religious, but possible incompetently religious man' – quoted by John Bowen in a 1959 essay reprinted in William Nelson (ed.), *William Golding's Lord of the Flies: A Source Book* (New York, 1963) p. 57.

25. See, specifically, 'The Hope of Pessimism', a long essay written by Gissing in 1882 and published for the first time by Pierre Coustillas in *George Gissing. Essays and Fiction* (Baltimore, 1970). But the deaths of Biffen and Reardon in *New Grub Street* illustrate the same attitude.

26. This article was written before I even heard of the appearance of *Darkness Visible* (1979). After reading that truly impressive novel, I see no reason to modify my conclusion that the author was and is starkly pessimistic about both the modern world and the nature of man.

Frank Kermode   On *The Spire* (1964)

. . . With the other novels in our head we can of course see how [*The Spire*] fits in the sequence: it is 'late', it is less assertive as to its possible meaning than *Lord of the Flies*; it has the later density, indeed fierceness, of language, and the power to generate meanings internally – meanings that grow out of the fiction and are not imposed from without. Consequently its themes are occult, as in *Free Fall*.

The Spire tells the story of Jocelin, Dean of some cathedral, and his efforts to realise a vision and a vow by building on to his church a 400-foot spire. That is all. And we see the entire action not so much through the eyes as over the shoulder of Jocelin; such facts as where the money came from, and what other interested parties think about the crazy dean, we gather by using the corners of our eyes. It is sometimes, for Golding's other books, both easy and useful to know his point of departure; nobody is the worse for understanding how *Lord of the Flies* is related to Ballantyne's *The Coral Island*, or for taking note of the epigraph of *The Inheritors*, which is from H. G. Wells's *Outline of History* and congratulates *homo sapiens* on his successful campaign against the Neanderthals. Here we are not told of any similar starting point; but Mr Golding must have got up the subject of how to build a spire, and the one he has in mind is Salisbury.[1] He makes the spire 400 feet high – Salisbury is a little over that – and the highest in England, as Jocelin wants it to be. It is surmounted by a capstone and a cross, as Salisbury spire is. It is octagonal, with a skin of diminishing thickness, and has no orthodox foundation, like Salisbury, of which it has been said that the dangers and difficulties of adding the spire were enough to frighten any man in his senses from trying it. Iron bands strengthen the structure. The four columns over which the spire was raised settled or bent in Salisbury, as in the book, and the spire at once slipped out of its true perpendicular, as here. In short, this is basically the spire at Salisbury. There was even a twelfth-century bishop called Jocelin. Despite some topographical mystification, the scene is consistent with this, and especially the Hanging Stones, which must be Stonehenge. And although it is no business of ours, Mr Golding lives near Salisbury. I don't know exactly where he got the facts about the mason's craft, however.[2]

In outline the story tells how the making good of the vision entails endlessly disagreeable and unforeseeable discoveries. It seemed simple enough; yet it has sordid material causes, unsuspected sexual motives; and it can be realised only in the teeth of technical obstacles which a sane man would regard as prohibitive. The cathedral being a bible in stone, the spire will be the Apocalypse; but it is also a human body and the spire its erect phallus. It all depends upon how your attention is focused. As Dean Jocelin himself observes, 'the mind touches all things with law, yet deceives itself as easily as a child'. The opening paragraph shows us Jocelin laughing, shaking his head so that a glory consumes and exalts Abraham, Isaac and God; his ways of looking, the moods of his mind, make and unmake vision and sacrifice. At this point Jocelin controls a manageable glory. But there is the question of the foundations, the palpitating human substratum that must maintain this glorious erection. And to its splendour the church is sacrificed, defiled by pagan workmen. Obscenely superstitious, they work as if taking part in some pagan rite. When they pry up the slabs at the crossways, it is clear that there are no foundations.

Against the will of the other principal persons, against the skilled advice of the master builder, Jocelin forces the business on; whatever the foundations of the spire – whether you take them to be mud, or the corrupt money of his aunt – he will have his four hundred feet and his cross with its Holy Nail, a diagram of prayer. Rain water in the excavations finds the corpses and makes the church foul; the master builder seduces the wife of a church servant; the spire seems founded on human filth, the earth 'a huddle of noseless men grinning upward'. The workmen fool about with the model spire obscenely between their legs; but the vision persists, even in the crossways, above the pit itself: 'Here, where the pit stinks, I received what I

received.' The four slender pillars are not divine but human
lovers, founded precariously on filth; they sing in agony under
the growing weight. The church servant disappears, and
Jocelin finds pagan mistletoe in the crossways – a typical
Golding narrative device, to issue in a revelation as horrible as
the recognition of Beatrice in the madhouse of *Free Fall*. Jocelin
fares forward: 'the folly isn't mine. It's God's Folly. . . . Out of
some deep place comes the command to do what makes no
sense at all – to build a ship on dry land; to sit among the
dunghills; to marry a whore.'

Whereas Jocelin thinks of each new foot of the building as a
godsent challenge to his strength personally to uphold the
structure, the master builder has material problems; he devises
a steel band to hold the outward thrust of the spire. Each is
clear about the cost, in life and lust and increase of foulness, of
this 'unruly member'. The mason's mistress dies for it – a
violent death in childbirth, Golding's recurrent figure for
violence and creation. 'This have I done for my true love',
thinks Jocelin with only apparent inconsequence. The
workmen desert for pagan midsummer fire festivals, and
Jocelin's own unruly member is tormented by the memory of
the dead woman. Reporting to the Visitor from Rome, he
presents himself – filthy, crazy – as 'Dean of the cathedral
church of Our Lady', the church he has desecrated, deprived of
services, made the scene of deadly lust. His spire is finished, the
Nail driven in; it is at once half-destroyed in a storm. And yet,
though built imperfectly, in folly and anguish, it is (he thinks in
hubris) a spire of prayer. Then the angel strikes him.[3] He has
brought ruin and loathing on himself and on the master builder
and the church; he can see only the hopeless conflict between
the kind of love he thought he had, and the kind that really
made the vision, so that the red hair of the dead woman hangs
between him and heaven, preventing prayer. On his deathbed
he finds a formula for this: 'a tangle of hair, blazing among the
stars; and the great club of his spire lifted towards it . . . that's
the explanation if I had time . . . Berenice.' The antinomies of
love are reconciled there; Jocelin's final gesture of assent is not
to the priests around his deathbed, but to the beautiful maimed
spire.

So much of the story one can tell without giving anything important away; such is the nature of Golding's power. It derives from patterns assumed by the language of the book from certain figures I haven't even mentioned: a tent, a net, a tree, as well as the mistletoe berry. Like *Lord of the Flies* it could be called a fable; but it is not a diagram. We are not to think of a prayer-spire and a phallus-spire, of Christian and pagan, devotion and lust, vision and graft. All these antinomies swirl together in the tormented mind of Jocelin, and in ours. We are even allowed to see how a deaf-mute carver understands Jocelin, and how the sacrist, a jealous, embittered, even venal man, is properly shocked by the pagan outrages on the holy vessels in his care; but Golding eschews the deliberate double vision which constitutes the plot of his first three books. Scholarly enquirers will have to look hard for a scenario here. Or, indeed, for a simple issue. Jocelin's dying thought is this: 'There is no innocent work. God only knows where God may be.' But that is not quite the point; nor is the suicide failure of the master builder (who, having gained weight by drinking, miscalculates at last the breaking strain of a rafter). Whether the vision was innocent or not, the technique sound or not, the spire is still there at the end, damaged but beautiful.[4]

Briefly then, this is a book about vision and its cost. It has to do with the motives of art and prayer, the phallus turned spire; with the deceit, as painful to man as to God, involved in structures which are human but have to be divine, such as churches and spires. But because the whole work is a dance of figurative language, such an account of it can only be misleading. It requires to be read with unremitting attention, and, first time perhaps, very little pleasure. It is second-period Golding; the voice is authoritative but under strain. The style might have been devised by some severe recluse for translating the Old Testament; it is entirely modern, without the slightest trace of god-wottery, yet it is almost unnaturally free of any hint of slang – a modern colloquial English but spoken only by one man.

Trying to characterise the dry hot urgency of this prose, I found myself unexpectedly thinking of a musician: of Vaughan Williams in the mood of *Job*. The parallel has some use, I feel.

The ballet for which this music was written was based on the
Blake engravings – the Old Testament in an extremely
heterodox interpretation. The music is in the full voice of
Vaughan Williams's already slightly archaic but fully
idiomatic, mere English, pentatonic manner; it goes directly to
the large statement about good and evil: Satan falling, Elihu
beautiful, the sons of the morning at their sarabande. Vaughan
Williams had some of the sensitive bluffness, much of the true
privacy, of Golding; and he was another late starter who
continually experimented but stayed out of touch with the
contemporary *avant-garde*. There is a squareness, a clumsiness;
but in some works – in *Job* especially, and in the later music
which remembers *Job* – we hear the clear strange tones of the
visionary whose idiom we can learn (a saxophone for the
comforters), and who speaks as directly as may be of good and
evil.

Golding writes rather like that. Look at this passage, chosen
quite at random:

> The evening turned green over the rim of the cup. Then the rim went black
> and shadows filled it silently so that before he was well aware of it, night had
> fallen and the faint stars come out. He saw a fire on the rim and guessed it was
> a haystack burning; but as he moved round the rim of the cone, he saw more
> and more fires round the rim of the world. Then a terrible dread fell on him,
> for he knew these were the fires of Midsummer Night, lighted by the
> devil-worshippers out on the hills. Over there, in the valley of the Hanging
> Stones, a vast fire shuddered brightly. All at once he cried out, not in terror
> but in grief. For he remembered his crew of good men, and he knew why they
> had knocked off work and where they were gone.

The 'cone' is the unfinished spire; we note how unashamedly
the sentence passes from its rim to the easy grandeur of 'the rim
of the world'. We might regret 'terrible dread', and yet it is
somehow purged by the absolute plainness of reference
elsewhere, by 'knocked off work', for instance. The last
sentence might seem altogether too artless were it not that on
this very page the whole strange plot is undergoing a subtle
change of movement, modulating into violence.

It is a prose for violence. All Golding's books are violent; as I
say, his basic figure for terror, violence and bloody creation is
childbirth. As such it is used in this book, and it breaks out of

the language into the plot. This is part of a private vision; and one might hazardously conjecture that this novel, like some of its predecessors, is as much about Golding writing a novel as about anything else. But one need not believe that to agree that it is deeply personal. It gives one some idea of the nature of this writer's gift that he has written a book about an expressly phallic symbol to which Freudian glosses seem entirely irrelevant. It is remote from the mainstream, potent, severe, even forbidding. And in its way it is a marvel. . . .

SOURCE: extract from a review of *The Spire* in the *New York Review of Books* (30 April 1964), pp. 3–4; subsequently incorporated in the essay 'The Later Golding' in *Continuities* (London, 1968), pp. 189–94.

NOTES

[Renumbered and reorganised from the original – Ed.]

1. [Ed.] See, however, the novelist's remarks about Salisbury, quoted in the essay on Golding's Sources (Part Two, above). In the same interview with Jack I. Biles, Golding says: '. . . in any case, my book doesn't necessarily have to be about Salisbury, does it? I deliberately knocked a couple of transepts off Salisbury Cathedral in order to be able to have chapter and verse for its not being.'

2. In fact, Mr Golding worked it all out himself, simply walking round the Cathedral and asking himself how *he* would have done it.

3. Tuberculosis of the spine, it appears.

4. [Ed.] For an interpretation arguing, from the implications of the text, that Jocelin's vision was one of 'destructiveness', not innocence, see Avril Henry's preliminary discussion of *The Spire* in her essay on *The Pyramid*, below. She brings out here a crucial element in Golding's 'obvious and obscure structure': Jocelin's abstention from Confession.

David Skilton   On *The Spire*   (1969)

The chief danger with Golding's novels is that they invite interpretation. The critic is tempted to obscure their literary qualities in a mass of quasi-philosophical speculation, or ruin their artistic integrity for pseudo-anthropological and pantopragmatic purposes of his own. It is true that in *Lord of the Flies*, *The Inheritors* and *Pincher Martin*, Golding does raise important questions about free will versus determinism, and about the nature of fallen man, while *Free Fall* is indeed a conscious quest by its narrator – one might say self-conscious – to find out when it was he fell from innocence, and made the crucial decision that left him no longer free. Because the answers to such questions as these in Golding's books are complex, even equivocal, his novels give the impression of being difficult to grasp, intellectually. And they are hard to understand if regarded purely as problems demanding and admitting of satisfactory solutions.

The Inheritors, *Pincher Martin*, *Free Fall* and *The Spire* are often regarded as quite difficult reading, *The Spire* in particular being thought of as almost willfully obscure; and the obstacles the reader meets with on the way seem at first to have delayed adequate recognition of it. The difficult thing to decide on first reading *The Spire* is whether it is exceedingly obvious or extremely subtle. It is a novel which absolutely demands to be read twice, and on the second reading it turns out to be neither, but, rather, a dense book that requires a certain amount of effort of penetration. The paradoxical impression of simplicity and complexity that one has at first arises from three fairly obvious qualities in Golding's writing. The first of these is the nature of Golding's vision of the world, which is a complex vision, in which a number of conflicting ideas or philosophies exist in tension. There are for Golding no simple, straightforward answers to the question of what is man's nature; yet the mutually opposed ideas his novels contain are often quite familiar in themselves, becoming complex only in their coexistence and presentation.

The second difficulty is stylistic, and arises from what it is usual to call the poetic intensity of Golding's writing. Alternating with passages of an almost startling lucidity, there are sections obscure enough to demand re-reading, and it is an obvious obstacle to the popular success of *The Spire* in particular that it cannot be fully grasped at one straightforward reading.

There is though a verbal magic in Golding which is quite convincing – so captivating in fact that the only fear the reader has at the end of one of his books is that perhaps it has all been a conjuring trick; that the Golding glamour has been cast again, and some subtle feat of legerdemain concealed. It will be the purpose of this article to show that this is not so, that the effect of *The Spire* is produced by careful artistic structuring and not by a trick at the reader's expense; but the fear is hard to dispel because the writing gives the impression of being almost too careful. Golding has such control, and seems so conscious of exactly what he is doing, that there is the terrible possibility that he is laughing at us all the time.

The third difficulty in reading Golding concerns narrative point of view in the novels, which is of such overwhelming importance that it is almost the same thing as to say their subject matter. He excels in presenting a story through the eyes of a person whose mentality is quite alien to the reader's own. This may be the Neanderthal man, Lok, in *The Inheritors*, or Dean Jocelin in *The Spire*; or it may be a modern, urban man, as average and sensual as ever was, yet *in extremis*, like the drowning sailor who is Pincher Martin. These persons through whom we see the action have quite different thought processes from ours: the Neanderthal men have no words for abstract concepts in their language; Jocelin is a visionary and (we are forced to consider) possibly mad. But there is more to it than this. These characters are, on the factual level, simply not reliable informants as to what is going on around them. They themselves do not understand what they see, and the reader must go with them through their process of discovering the true significance of the events they witness. Hence the impression of denseness and obscurity.

The difficulty inherent in analysing Golding's 'message' is only a pseudo-complexity, although approaching his work from a quasi-philosophical point of view provides plenty of fun for all the critical family, because the process of interpretation is never-ending. One simple, straightforward account can never be final, for it is always possible to show that alternative interpretations are at least as viable. The alternative 'messages' in the novels exist in tension, so that one does not overcome the others. Man is neither a fully rational nor a fully irrational being; he is ruled entirely neither by his own will nor by fate. The problems posed by human existence admit of no such simple solutions, and Golding proves this by presenting conflicting ideas in tension, in a concrete situation, in such a way that it is the concrete situation that is of prime importance, and hence the novel itself, as an artifact. With no author does the process of interpretation leave a greater sense of inadequacy than with Golding, because the most striking thing about his novels is their 'thereness', and if ever a writer produced works that seemed solid – almost palpable – it was surely he. The work of art *per se* is the most important thing, and the various interpretations merely different ways of looking at the central reality it presents. Interpret the novels how we will, there remains Golding's poetic vision, which is unassailable in terms of message and meaning. His persons and things are primarily persons and things, and do not stand for something else.

The Spire is a novel in which the author has clearly expended a great deal of energy in building up a world, and relied to an unusually small degree on the reader's foreknowledge derived from the world around him. In *Pincher Martin* the process is explicit, for the whole novel is an effort of creation in Pincher's mind. Yet in *Pincher Martin* the strain of maintaining the illusion shows through, and there is a sense that the whole thing is a little too contrived for perfect satisfaction. *The Inheritors* and *The Spire*, however, are completely successful in this respect, each being a *tour de force* in the total construction of an imaginary world.

Set in the Middle Ages, *The Spire* is the story of the erection of a huge, 400-foot tower and spire on an English cathedral. It is told from the point of view of Jocelin, the dean of the cathedral, through whose eyes everything significant is seen, so that the novelist's narrative persona is almost entirely suppressed. Many years earlier Jocelin has had a vision of the spire as a 'crowning glory' surmounting his cathedral, and completing the 'diagram of prayer' it represents. Only as he pushes on with his ambition does he come to understand his own past, his motives, and exactly what he is doing to the people he involves in his enterprise. It is this progress of understanding that is the chief movement in the novel, so that here, as in *The Inheritors*, point of view is all-important, and indistinguishable from the subject matter: the significance of both books lies in the way the events are regarded. Both Jocelin and Lok are far from 'reliable' observers, and everything the reader is presented with is seen refracted through their particular consciousnesses.

As the building of the tower and spire proceeds, Jocelin discovers that he is using tainted money obtained from his aunt, the Lady Alison, who was mistress of the previous king, and who is trying to buy a tomb for herself within sight of the High Altar. He is employing an 'army' of pagan workmen, who desecrate the cathedral with their noise, dirt and language, and with their pagan rites. When a pit is dug under the crossways of the cathedral, and it is discovered that there are no foundations to speak of – that the whole building floats on mud, on a raft of brushwood – and as the pillars that must bear the weight of the new spire are seen to be woefully inadequate, the workmen refuse to go on. But Jocelin has the master mason, Roger, in his power, for Roger cannot leave. He is trapped in what Jocelin sees as a 'tent', a net, of sexual involvement with Goody, the wife of the cathedral factotum. The factotum, Pangall, is persecuted by the workmen because he is a cripple, and – a fact unknown consciously to Jocelin – impotent. The work is forced on, and when mud begins to bubble up out of the pit, like a terrible threat from the dark regions, the army of workmen goes wild and ritually murders Pangall, burying him crouched under the crossways, to bear the weight of the fabric and of their fear.

It is not so much the ritual murder in itself that is so interesting – although many people seem to think of Golding as a sort of 'anthropological' writer – but the place of the ritual in the structure of the novel. In a sense, it provides the structure of the novel quite as much as the construction of the spire does, for the action of the book is really Jocelin's progress from ignorance to enlightenment. After the first reading – and *The Spire* demands to be read more than once – the gripping, but nevertheless spurious tension created by the doubt as to whether the spire will be got up or not, is replaced by the far greater interest of Jocelin's slow-dawning realisation of the nature of the events he has instigated. Although he saw much of what happened at the time of the ritual killing, the dean does not at first understand the significance of his perceptions, but as the book proceeds, he comes stage by stage to a comprehension not only of what happened then, but of just what he himself is doing and why.

As he drives Roger Mason and his army onwards and upwards, he is tormented by the devil in sexual dreams, and driven on by an ambiguous good-bad angel at his back, who finally strikes him down in the form of tuberculosis of the spine. Throughout he has lent strength to the slim pillars from his own back, and throughout he is identified with the cathedral. He has a dream in which he sees himself as the building:

> ... Satan was permitted to torment him during the night by a meaningless and hopeless dream. It seemed to Jocelin that he lay on his back in his bed; and then he was lying on his back in the marshes, crucified, and his arms were the transepts. . . . People came to jeer and torment him, there was Rachel, there was Roger, there was Pangall, and they know the church had no spire nor could have any.   [pp. 64–5][1]

This dream of impotence refers back to a phallic image on the second page of the text, where a model of the cathedral is a man on his back:

> The nave was his legs placed together, the transepts on either side were his arms outspread. The choir was his body; and the Lady Chapel . . . was his head. And now also, springing, projecting, bursting, erupting from the heart of the building, there was its crown and majesty, the new spire.   [p. 8]

Jocelin's consumption of the spine finally strikes him when he discovers that the pillars are not solid stone, but filled with rubble [p. 188]. And when in the last chapter he is lying drugged with poppy, he is again the cathedral of the opening pages, when an opening is made, joining the inside to the outside, and he thinks, 'Now I lay a hand on the very body of my church. Like a surgeon, I take my knife to the stomach drugged with poppy' [p. 13].

What happens to the building happens to Jocelin too. The novel traces the forming in his consciousness of connections between parts of himself which he previously believed to be separate, just as the work on the cathedral unites the inside and the outside, which 'yesterday, or a Hail Mary ago, . . . were a quarter of a mile apart' [p. 12]. The novel too is 'doing the unthinkable', joining 'earth to heaven' [p. 69].

'I never guessed in my folly', Jocelin thinks, 'that there would be a new lesson at every level, and a new power' [p. 108]. But there is, and the power is the power to destroy as much as the power to create. If Jocelin has any connection with Ibsen's master builder Solness, or with others of Ibsen's protagonists, it is in this, that he is driven on to the heights, and in the process must inevitably destroy himself and those around him, by denying other human faculties.

By the end of *The Spire*, Jocelin has come to realise exactly what happened to Pangall in the violence under the crossways, and with each step in his growing awareness, he has come to discover other things as well. Something he knew subconsciously breaks through into his consciousness – that he knew Pangall was impotent and arranged Goody's marriage with him accordingly, because his own interest in her was powerfully sexual. By the time the spire is topped off, Jocelin has destroyed Pangall and Goody, and Roger Mason, and almost destroyed the cathedral itself as a place of worship, for no services have been held or candles burnt in it for months. Yet the action is ambivalent, neither wholly good nor wholly bad, for he alone had the faith (or was it the madness?) necessary to crown the cathedral so gloriously. When he dies himself at the end of the book, it is in a bewitched condition, haunted by Goody and her tumbling mass of red hair, and entangled in the tendrils of a plant of sexuality. It is not certain even at this point whether Golding wants us to believe that he is saved and has found the ability to pray, or whether he remains, as he says himself, like a building with rats in the cellarage [pp. 210, 213, 219]. Golding's novels never have one unequivocal 'message'. As Jocelin says in *The Spire*, 'That's too simple, like every other explanation. That gets nowhere near the root' [p. 195].

What *The Spire* does achieve is a revelation like that made by Roger's wife, Rachel, who 'stripped the business of living down to where horror and farce took over' [p. 59]; so that at the end of the novel it is necessary to consider the whole man, 'the whole building, cellarage and all', and what 'the cellarage [the subconscious] knew' [p. 213]. At the same time, the conflicts of the book are subsumed into a pair of simple, radiant images which constitute an equivocal vision of natural yet magical beauty. In his last extremity, Jocelin gets up from his deathbed to go out in search of Roger Mason, and passing through the dean's yard, he is struck by the scent of an appletree, which gives him an instant of 'wild hope'. He sees the blossom as 'a cloud of angels flashing in the sunlight', and he understands that 'there was more to the appletree than one branch. It was there beyond the wall, bursting up with cloud and scatter, laying hold of the earth and the air, a fountain, a marvel, an appletree' [pp. 204–5] – like the spire, the cathedral, and man himself. Then he has a glimpse of a kingfisher, 'all the blue of the sky condensed to a winged sapphire', that flies once, never to return. 'All the same, he said to himself, I was lucky to see it. No one else saw it.' At the moment of his death, he sees the spire 'rushing upward to some point at the sky's end, and with a silent cry', and he realises, 'Now – I know nothing at all'. He dies, 'in the tide, flying like a bluebird, struggling, shouting, screaming to leave behind the words of magic and incomprehension – *It's like the appletree!*' [p. 223].

So his end is both visionary and equivocal, like his life, closing on the unresolved tension of the paradox of his blindness versus his privilege in seeing the vision of all – 'I was lucky to see it. No one else saw it' [p. 205].

The whole structure and the chief importance of *The Spire* lie in the way Jocelin looks at his world. The time structure and the imagery of the book are entirely Jocelin's. In respect of narrative point of view, *Lord of the Flies* is elementary Golding. Part of the action is seen through Ralph's eyes, part through Simon's, and part through the eyes of an outside narrative persona. But in *The Spire*, as in *The Inheritors*, Golding works through a single refracting consciousness, and the value of the novel lies to a very large extent in his ability to involve us so absolutely in the working of a totally alien mind. Far from rendering *The Inheritors* and *The Spire* irrelevant, this foreignness is the basis of their artistic value, and of any moral value they possess, in that they involve us from the inside with something that is so very unlike ourselves, persuading us to accept ways of thought different from our own.

The sequence of the physical events in *The Spire* is very straightforward, and in this respect the novel displays a more subtle control than *Free Fall*, where the narrative is arranged in a particular chronological order, to make a point about the narrator's life. The story is constantly turning back on itself in search of its own significance. *The Spire* works in much the same way, in as far as it is an inquiry into the meaning of Jocelin's life; but the quest is set in a straightforward account of a sequence of physical events, and largely concerns these events. The chronology of the events is purely linear, while Dean Jocelin's understanding of them works on a quite different scale, determining to a large extent the reader's comprehension too, since the reader cannot see anything Jocelin does not see, and can by the nature of things only understand a very little that he does not understand.

There are in fact three time scales working together in *The Spire*, each producing its own interest and suspense.[2] The first is the chronological ordering of the events of building the spire: page by page it gets higher, and everything about the operation is described in its due, logical place, relying for its fascination on the details of medieval building techniques, and on the doubt as to the final outcome of the project. Then there are Jocelin's discoveries about his past, long before the time when the novel opens, which follow the pattern of the revelations in Ibsen's plays from *The Pillars of Society* onwards. In rather the same way as the Alvings' respectability in *Ghosts*, for example, is shown to be based on rottenness and sham, it is revealed that Jocelin originally owed his preferment to Lady Alison's whim when she was lying in bed with the late king, and that he was, moreover, quite unqualified for his appointment. Jocelin, and he alone in the Chapter, has been quite unaware of this fact, and this revelation forms his first progress of understanding.

The third time system of the novel is Jocelin's other development of comprehension, this time of the events connected with the building of the spire, and specifically the ritual killing of Pangall and the significance of his own feelings for Goody. This sequence of mental events is indicated in the summary of the plot above. The ritual killings occurs on page 90, where the events are seen, as always, through Jocelin's eyes:

He was struck by a gust of laughter. . . . The noises were as confused as the lights that swirled in his head. The place was a mass of brown tunics, leather jerkins, blue tunics, clothbound legs, wallets of leather, beards and teeth. . . . He knew this was some nightmare; since things happened and stuck in the eye as if seen by flashes of lightening [sic].   [p. 89]

As always, his perceptions are immediate and concrete, and unanalysed.

In an apocalyptic glimpse of seeing, he caught how a man danced forward to Pangall, the model of the spire projecting obscenely from between his legs . . . he could not see, but only heard how Pangall broke – He heard the long wolfhowl of the man's flight down the south aisle, heard the rising, the hunting noise of the pack that raced after him.   [p. 90]

He sees Goody clutching a pillar, her red hair hanging free, her dress torn, turning her 'white, contracted mouth . . . towards Roger on this side of the pit, his arms spread from his side in anguish and appeal, in acknowledgement of consent and defeat'. The image 'was printed on his eye forever. Whenever there should be darkness and no thought, the picture would come back.' Then he is crushed under the weight of bodies.

Jocelin hardly understands what he has seen and heard, and in the next chapter he is 'locked in his head with only a few things. These few things sorted themselves endlessly but never arrived at any order' [p. 91]. He believes Pangall to have run away and deserted Goody, but finding a few pages later a berry and a twig on the floor, he turns to worrying about the seasoning of the wood the men are using. That is on page 95, and he does not express finally what has happened to Pangall until his last interview with Roger Mason at the very end of the book when he talks about the spire:

'What holds it up, Roger? I? The nail? Does she, or do you? Or is it poor Pangall, crouched beneath the crossways, with a sliver of mistletoe between his ribs?'   [p. 212]

At the first reading, this produces a sudden shock, for it is far from obvious how Jocelin has reached this point of understanding, because the reader's mind has been occupied with many subjects throughout the book. A second reading, however, reveals that he has throughout been sorting his thoughts, and making more and more order out of past events. For the first two-thirds of the novel, he does not truly follow what is happening around him, but as the building progresses, there is indeed a new lesson at every level, until on Midsummer Night the workmen pack up early and leave Jocelin alone up the spire. As darkness falls, he sees the bale fires of the pagan celebrations way out on the plain, and says to himself,

'It's another lesson. The lesson for this height. Who could have foreseen that this was part of the scheme? Who could have known that at this height the thing I thought of as a stone diagram of prayer would lift up a cross and fight eye to eye with the fires of the Devil?' [pp. 155–6]

Then he thinks of Goody and of the workmen, and (like Ralph at the end of *Lord of the Flies*) 'wept bitterly without knowing what he wept for unless it was the sins of the world'. Then his mind gets to work on its own, as 'a host of memories flew together. He watched, powerless to stop as they added to each other.' Then he feels suddenly cold, 'remembering himself watching the floor down there, where among the dust and rubble a twig with a brown, obscene berry lay against his foot. . . . "Mistletoe!" ' He rushes down the tower, 'and at the crossways, the replaced paving stones were hot to his feet with all the fires of hell' [pp. 155–7]. This moment in the tower is the turning point in his realisation, for it is the moment at which he first understands what is actually happening at that very moment. At this point the two opposite chronologies intersect, and from now on, as time passes and the events move forward, his understanding progresses in the contrary direction, until, at last, he knows exactly what happened that day at the crossways, just how he has destroyed the people around him, and how his phallic ambition to erect the spire is connected to his interest in Goody.

Thus even the time structure depends upon the narrative point of view, because the development of the novel is totally shaped by Jocelin's consciousness.

Imagery too plays a key role in the presentation of the subject matter through Jocelin's refracting consciousness, because, in this narrative technique, the imagery is his, and not used by a narrator to express or convey Jocelin's states of mind and perceptions. That is to say that although it is a third-person novel as far as the grammatical person of the narrative verbs is concerned, the author's narrative persona has been suppressed with a skill for which Golding stands almost alone. The process of suppression involves presenting Jocelin's thoughts and perceptions directly, without explanation or interpretation, so that in the quotation given above of his vision of the appletree, for example, the reader is not helped by being told in the first place that the vision of angels is an appletree, because Jocelin's perception of it precedes the abstraction necessary to name the phenomenon in conventional words. This forces one to re-read certain passages, just as the interpretation of the events through Jocelin's consciousness forces one to reconsider the whole book.

The central symbol of the book is the spire itself, which has an obvious and explicit dual significance as on the one hand the completion of the 'diagram of prayer', crowning it and aspiring heavenwards; and on the other hand a phallus. The development of the novel can be traced through Jocelin's growing awareness of the phallic aspect, which is at first only subconscious, although obvious to the reader, who has the advantage of being able to interpret the symbol very easily in Freudian terms, and has thus for once an awareness denied to Jocelin. This conventional symbol is brilliantly integrated into the very texture of Jocelin's experience, to provide a *motif* which holds the novel tightly together. The spire is also a club, a hammer which destroys four people, an upward rushing towards the sky, 'a silent cry'; it is a slim girl, a plant, an upward waterfall, and it breaks 'all the way to infinity in cascades of exultation that nothing could trammel' [p. 223]. Most important, in its twin nature as praise and phallus, it unites the cellarage of man to his mind, and earth to heaven, like the hole in the cathedral roof, and like the novel itself.

There are in addition various clusters of images in the novel, which create Jocelin's world, while holding the book tightly together. One of them shall be briefly indicated: the group, gargoyles-eagle-raven-mayfly. The gargoyles on the cathedral 'burst out of the stone like boils or pimples, purging the body of sickness, ensuring by their self-damnation, the purity of the whole [p. 67]. In a drought they 'gaped as though they sought water in the dry air. There was no point of rest for them. They were in hell, could expect no less, that was all there was to it' [p. 97]. This is a conventional interpretation of the gargoyle, but these are also the terms in which Jocelin thinks of them, for he thinks in the patterns of his own medieval Christian culture. The gargoyles, however, also have a significance particular to this novel, because four heads of Jocelin in stone are to be built into the top of the new tower. The dumb man who carves them shows Jocelin with an aquiline nose, hair streaming back to give an impression of speed. 'An eagle, perhaps?' asks Jocelin. 'You are thinking of the Holy Spirit?' These heads connect with the other gargoyles, and with Jocelin's spire as 'a silent cry' as well:

Rushing on with the angels, the infinite speed that is stillness, hair blown back, straightened with the wind of the spirit, mouth open, not for uttering rainwater, but hosannas and hallelujahs.   [p. 24]

Lying on his deathbed, Jocelin sees himself in terms of these stone heads: 'Hair blown back by the wind of the spirit. Mouth open, not for uttering rainwater but for hosannahs' [p. 195].

The eagle nature of the heads refers them to a moment on top of the half-built tower when Jocelin looking up sees a great bird, and thinking of St John says, 'It is an eagle' [p. 107]. Typically his listener cannot understand that he is talking in emblematic terms of aspiration towards the throne of God, and that, as is natural in a visionary, he identifies with St John. His original vision of the spire reached a point in the sky where a bird sailed, and so this is the pinnacle of his ambitions. This by no means exhausts the significance of the birds, for those that glide over the cathedral are in fact ravens, and Jocelin contrasts himself with Roger Mason as a raven to a mayfly. The raven knows that the sun will rise tomorrow, but the mayfly can know nothing of tomorrow, as it only lives for one day. It can see only means, not ends. A reference to the mayfly also occurs on the fourth page of the novel, when particles of dust raised by the initial work on the paving of the cathedral 'turned over each other, or bounced all together, like mayfly in a breath of wind' [p. 10], so that the image gains by its association with the builders, the human agents of the erection of the spire.

There are several such clusters holding the vision of *The Spire* together, such as that including the fabric of praise, the maze woven by Goody's feet, the tent, the plant of sexual complication, and the appletree. And the function of these sequences of images is both to unify the work, and to form the connection between the animal and spiritual aspects of man.

One of the most striking features of *The Spire* is the intense realisation of light and darkness in it, forming a *motif* of dual, and sometimes equivocal, significance. The novel opens with Jocelin standing in the light of a stained-glass window: 'God the Father was exploding in his face with a glory of sunlight through painted glass' [p. 7]; and throughout the book the people Jocelin speaks with are seen moving into and out of the light, so that anything is visually realised as vividly as in any film. There is only light and shadow – hardly any half-light. Darkness descends with the rain and cloud, as the graves in the cathedral flood, and the mud at the bottom of the pit begins to work. But once the work on the tower progresses, there is light up there, while the nave remains in blackness. Then on Midsummer Night, Jocelin sees the bale fires from the plain round about, and realises that he is looking at the light that belongs to the devil, which his spire, raised up, must fight eye to eye with its cross.

Then there is the ambiguous light that is the power of the vision that drives him on for good or ill, and the light of his sudden flashes of perception of the events around the pit during the killing of Pangall. Finally there is the bright hair in the sky – Goody's hair – that cuts him off from heaven with its brilliance [p. 127]. In a wonderful moment of ironic insight, he sees the spire from his deathbed as a phallic club rising up towards the tangle of hair, and understanding at last the sexual aspect of his ambitions, says to himself, '. . . that's the explanation if I had time'. So he murmurs, 'Berenice', at which the priest with him asks, 'Saint?' Jocelin tries to laugh, having no strength left for explanations. He was seeing the constellation of the hair of Berenice shining in the sky [p. 221].

Another means by which Golding involves the reader in Jocelin's perceptions, and effects the total creation of the world of the novel, is by the use of synaesthetic devices, such as Jocelin's frequent seeing of sounds. On his deathbed the curious question, 'When you hear things, do you see them?' is merely the culmination of a long series of perceptions throughout the novel. He hears voices writing in the air, experiencing them visually at the same time. Father Adam's is like a pencil on a slate. Jocelin sees too the mark left in the air by the scream of a workman who falls from the tower, and he watches the sound of a whistle turn the corner past the deanery.[3]

By such devices, the reader is put inside Jocelin's experiences, and the unity of the novel is assured. Most of all, the use of synaesthesia, imagery and *motif*, and the careful time structuring of *The Spire*, make the novel an independent creation, demanding as little local reference as possible to the everyday world of the twentieth century.

SOURCE: essay in *Studies in the Literary Imagination*, II (Oct. 1969), pp. 45–56.

NOTES

[Reorganised and renumbered from the original – Ed.]

1. William Golding, *The Spire* (London, 1964), pp. 64–5. All subsequent citations are to this edition.

2. [Ed.] See also Avril Henry's discussion of 'time as a structural device' in *The Spire*, in her essay on *The Pyramid* immediately following.

3. See pp. 25, 46, 54, 61, 98, 194–5.

Avril Henry   'Time in *The Pyramid*'
(1969)

... With one exception [A. S. Byatt][1] reviewers of *The Pyramid*[2] seem to have underestimated Mr Golding's control of his material. It may be true that his novels 'tempt the critic to demonstrate his own cleverness by taking them apart and picking about among the debris' but at least such analysis will prevent our thinking the book 'no more than a jewel-case for ... Miss Dawlish' (as if it were a character-study in miniature) or that it consists of 'three stories, each shorter than the one before it'[3] when in fact the third section is longer than the second by eighteen pages – not even a large enough difference to make the book's central section form a small apex between two equal sides of a 'pyramid'.[4]

Mrs Byatt's perceptive review illuminates both the novelist's method and his choice of title. I shall turn later to the significance of the Pyramid. First I am concerned simply to provide a gloss on what Mrs Byatt has said of the novel's structure:

the dimension of mystery is shown in a series of brilliantly-placed *puns* or Freudian *doubles-entendres* – which are both very funny, and open up sudden, unexpected and savage depths of meaning.

Here apparent banality of style and subject-matter has not been taken at its remarkably unlovely face-value. An analysis of the series of events, the way in which they are 'brilliantly-placed', helps to reveal the complex pattern of ideas informing the book.

Like his symbols, Mr Golding's novel-structure is at once obvious and obscure. It is true that the three episodes of the book show Oliver adolescent, then in the Christmas vacation of his first year at Oxford, and finally some thirty years later.[5] But this is to ignore all the significant deviations from mere chronological treatment: carefully-planned deviations apparently dictated by the reminiscing mind in the manner we have become used to in *Pincher Martin* and *Free Fall*, which also examine aspects of human nature in 'the over-riding human necessity of finding a link between separate phenomena'.[6] Each of the three main sections is divided up by references to time. The divisions are of two kinds: major ones marked by flashback or 'flashforward', and minor ones marking the passage of days, weeks, terms or years.

Mr Golding has used time as a structural device before. In *Pincher Martin* there 'plays across the narrative chapters, in fact, another structure altogether: a kind of parody of the Divine Week of Creation, but ending at the beginning of the Seventh Day when the work of human hands must be set aside.'[7] The structure is functional, pointing the destructive nature of Pincher's experience.

A time-structure is also used in *The Spire*, and as it is a subtler use than that in the earlier novel, and helps us to understand the method in *The Pyramid*, I shall digress to examine it. *The Spire* moves us through two years: from the early Spring of the first to the Spring of the third. Each chapter but the last contains some indication of the month or season: indications which are frequent in the first year, less so in the second. There are two gaps in the succession of months. One occurs between chapters x and xi when Jocelin, who fell sick in August, leaves his bed in late Spring, and sees the appletree in blossom. His sickness of body absented him from the greatest season in the liturgical year: Lent and Easter. The other gap is earlier, in chapter vii, and the careful documenting of feasts and months which precedes it in chapters i – vi makes it more noticeable. In chapter vii, although the narrative through Jocelin's consciousness continues uninterrupted, mention of Lent and Easter is again omitted: on page 113 [ch. vi] it is December, but on page 152 [ch. viii] it is suddenly midsummer. All we have in ch. vii to remind us of Easter is Jocelin's painful memory of how he had seen Goody Pangall and Roger Mason in the 'tent' of their attraction for each other 'more than a year ago' [p. 137]. The account of that 'tent' is in two parts [ch. iii, pp. 58, 64; ch. iv, p. 69]. Between the two, mention is made of Jocelin's failure to go to confession [p. 67], the one annual Easter confession to omit which *automatically* excommunicates the defaulter – excludes him from all the channels of divine grace, with the exception of Confession, which are the Sacraments. In chapter VII the omission causes him pain [p. 137]; having remembered the past year, and the occasion of his first failure to be confessed, he addresses God: 'More than a year ago I . . .' but breaks off, not defining the pain or giving voice to the guilt. On page 147 he remembers that once *'there was God'*. When a month is next mentioned, on page 152, it is midsummer. Lent and Easter, so carefully described in the first year, have been left out. In the second year the *fact* of omitted confession is not mentioned: it is implied by the liturgical gap in Jocelin's consciousness, which we are made to share. If we are in any doubt at all about the nature of Jocelin's 'vision' this is the clearest indication of its destructiveness – for in this novel the values of the medieval setting are not undermined by the author. (I do not feel that such values are undermined in any of the novels, even in *The Pyramid.*[8])

In *Pincher Martin* and *The Spire*, then, a careful time-structure is used to underline the central statement of the novels. These examples not only warn us that Mr Golding's use of time, so stressed in *The Pyramid*, is likely to be very deliberate: they suggest the nature of the deliberation. A time-sequence is carefully established so that any alteration, omission or curtailment in it will be noticeable, and can be made to act as one of the many devices focusing the reader's attention.

To return to *The Pyramid*: Section One consists, at a narrative level, of the loveless relationship of Olly and Evie. The bulk of the section [pp. 1–100] covers a complete summer month, in which each day is accounted for, if not described: one month in Olly's eighteenth year; (by this I mean the year in which he was eighteen: the strictly correct numbering which would call this his nineteenth year is confusing in a context where numbers may themselves be significant). These first hundred pages constitute what I shall call 1(a). This apparently empty exactitude in accounting for each day directs our attention to the importance of time as a device in this novel, as in the two others cited above. We are made aware of an attention to detail which is at variance with an apparently casual narrative, and we are conditioned to notice breaks in continuity when they do occur. In order to 'make a mock of the arbitrary, enslaving time-stream'[9] the author must first make us aware of it.

But the day-by-day sequence also acts as a firm framework for an apparently mundane narrative which is in fact composed of carefully interwoven themes which recur throughout the book. To these I shall return. At present I am concerned only with the main outlines of the time-structure. Section One ends (p. 101) with the meeting of Olly, then at the end of his second Oxford year, and Evie: in other words it takes place *two years after* the events described in the first hundred pages. This meeting I shall call 1(b). It is not at first easy to see why the author created the time-gap here: why the accusation of rape which Evie makes must be against an Olly two years older. On first reading, the point is not even clear when Olly remarks (p. 106): 'the last time I had been in the Crown was with Mr De Tracy nearly two years before, a notable occasion'. This notable occasion is not described until the middle of Section Two.

The time-gap between 1(a) and 1(b): its function

These displaced pieces of the narrator's autobiography – the meeting with Evie in the Crown, and the mention of the meeting with De Tracy in the Crown – serve two simultaneous purposes in the novel. In this they are perhaps unusual. It is not uncommon to find flashbacks and 'flashforwards' which are functional in the time-sequence of a novel as, for example, in the ironic structures of [Conrad's] *Nostromo*; it is not uncommon to find them related significantly to the context of the chronological pattern of a protagonist's 'real' life, as for example in [Miller's] *Death of a Salesman* or [Aldous Huxley's] *Point Counter Point*. But in *The Pyramid* they function on a symbolic level in the sequence both of the novel *and* of the 'real' life. An outline, first of the sequence of events in the novel, and then of Oliver's 'real' life, with page references to the places where its parts are in fact described, will help to make this dual function clear and to clarify the ways in which the displacements draw our attention to major themes.

The book is in three sections:

Section One contains one time-gap and one flashback.

| Before Oxford | 1(a) | The affair of Olly and Evie; and the binoculars episode. |
| End 2nd year | 1(b) | **Olly and Evie in the Crown. Olly's reference to meeting De Tracy in the Crown: a flashback to earlier events, described later in Section Two.** |

Section Two is sequential narrative.

| End 1st Oxford term | 2(a) | Arrival at Stilbourne. |
| | 2(b) | Rehearsal and performance of *King of Hearts* during which **Olly meets De Tracy in the Crown**, and is shown photographs. |

Section Three

1963: Oliver adult	3(a)	Oliver visits Stilbourne.
	3(b)	Flashback to his 3rd, 6th, 10th, 17th and 18th years.
	3(c)	Flashback to events in each of his Oxford years, ending with Bounce's nakedness and its consequences.
1963: Oliver adult	3(d)	Return to Stilbourne.

In 'real-life' chronology 1(a), 1(b), and 2 fit somewhere into 3. All of 2 and some of 3 must precede 1(b). The 'real-life' sequence is thus as follows:

Childhood and adolescence:

Age 3	p. 164	Sec. 3	Olly sees old Mr Dawlish break phonograph.
Age 6	p. 165	Sec. 3	Olly first meets Bounce: first violin-lesson, first car-ride.
Age 10	p. 183	Sec. 3	Bounce's suffering: Henry and the garage.
Age 17	p. 192	Sec. 3	Academic takes precedence over musical work.
Age 18	pp. 1–100	Sec. 1(a)	Affair of Olly and Evie.
Age 18	p. 198	Sec. 3	Olly packs for Oxford.

Oxford:		
End 1st term p. 112 Sec. 2		*King of Hearts*; **Olly and De Tracy: the Crown.**
End 2nd term p. 200 Sec. 3		Olly meets Bounce in crashed car outside Stilbourne.
		Olly at Oxford, reads of her Dangerous Driving.
End 2nd *year* p. 206 Sec. 3		Olly at home: Bounce goes out naked.
	p. 101 Sec. 1(b)	**Olly and Evie at the Fair and the Crown.**
Last year	p. 208 Sec. 3	Olly's parents, *at Oxford*, tell Olly Bounce was 'put away'.
After War and some years of peace:		
1948 plus	p. 208 Sec. 3	Oliver and family at Stilbourne. Bounce's animals.
1963	p. 157 Sec. 3	Oliver, aged about 45, at Henry's garage and Bounce's grave: he remembers past events.
	p. 212 Sec. 3	Same place: Oliver understands himself, and leaves.

We can now see why there is a two-year time-gap before 1(b). Evie's public accusation of rape made in the Crown serves a dual function in the two sequences – the novel and 'real-life'. In the context of the *novel's* sequence it is expressly related to two other examples of public exhibition or private exposure, and so draws our attention to one of the novel's major themes. First, the day-by-day account of the affair between Olly and Evie – 1(a) – has just ended with Olly's father watching their copulation through binoculars. Second, as they enter the Crown, Oliver/the narrator refers to the 'notable occasion' when he had been in the pub with De Tracy, two years before [p. 106]. On this occasion, described in Section Two, De Tracy, spurred on by Olly's naive desire to know 'the truth of things' [p. 148], shows the uncomprehending young man photographs of his, De Tracy's, transvestism.

But in the 'real' chronology, Olly's public shaming in the Crown is preceded by Bounce's naked exit into the street: another 'public exhibition'. No wonder he is horrified by the publicity he is given: he has seen Stilbourne 'turn its corporate back' [pp. 207–8] on a victim of scandal. Later, in this third year at Oxford (though still only on page 208), he learns the full consequences: Bounce was 'put away'. The displaced portion, 1(b), therefore works in both contexts, narrative and natural.

Mrs Byatt notes the link between the binoculars episode, De Tracy's photographs, and Bounce's nakedness: '. . . each of the three episodes culminates in a display of post-lapsarian nakedness.' This is true: the sections culminate emotionally in these scenes, without ending on them. But 'post-lapsarian' does not really define these 'nakednesses'. Their effects are very varied. To Olly's horror [p. 101] Evie remains unchanged by the binoculars episode which she engineered. De Tracy's 'revelation of truth' is not even understood by his audience, and so both shame and disappointment drive him to drunkenness in which he, like Olly at the end of Section One when he is 'drowned by the Stilbourne tide', is found under the glare of the sodium light by the Town Hall. Bounce naked in the street is Bounce for once 'calm and happy, with a relaxed, smiling face' [p. 216]. But if the effect on Evie of her accusation of rape is very little (she has nothing to lose in connection with that particular reputation), her reaction to Olly's innocent (or is it defensive or vengeful?) salutation 'Bottoms Up' is remarkable. We recall her reaction to Olly's discovering the marks of Wilmot's flagellation on her bottom: a painful flush, itself recalling Olly's own blush when his mere intentions with regard to Evie are almost discovered by Henry [pp. 37–8], and a passionate desire to avoid publication of his discovery. This is what prompts her to 'betray' Olly publicly with a double lie: she was not raped, and she was eighteen, not fifteen, when Olly first had her – though she was fifteen when she first took pity on the ghastly Wilmot. The effect of this betrayal on Olly is apparent not only at the time, but later in the book. He does not wait to be socially 'put away'. He leaves the village, to return only when equipped with money, wife and children; with the only witness of the 'rape' – his father – dead, Olly is beyond scandal. (This absence from the village is presumably why we are told that Olly is at Oxford, not Stilbourne, when he learns of Bounce's being 'put away'. In 'real' chronology this news follows his visit to the Crown with Evie.) . . .

SOURCE: extract from 'William Golding: *The Pyramid*', *Southern Review: An Australian Journal of Literary Studies*, III (1968–9), pp. 5–10.

NOTES

1. A. S. Byatt, *New Statesman* (2 June 1967), p. 761.
2. William Golding, *The Pyramid* (London, 1967). All references are to the Faber editions.
3. M. Haltrecht, *Sunday Times* (4 June 1967), p. 28.
4. P. Barker, *The Times* (1 June 1967), p. 7, also believes the title to refer to the novel's triple structure.
5. R. Baldick, *Daily Telegraph* (1 June 1967), p. 21. See also the anonymous reviewer in *Times Literary Supplement* (1 June 1967), p. 481: 'Among these three episodes there are certain connections of character and scene, but these do not make for a very tightly or very elaborately structured book.'
6. W. Golding, in an essay 'Copernicus', *The Hot Gates and Other Occasional Pieces* (London, 1965), p. 31.
7. M. Kinkead-Weekes & I. Gregor, *William Golding: A Critical Study* (London, 1967), p. 135.
8. H. Cixous, *Le Monde* (26 July 1967), supplement p. 1, thinks *The Pyramid* destructive.
9. 'The Glass Door', *The Hot Gates*, p. 141.

David Skilton   *The Pyramid* and Comic Social Fiction   (1978)

In being a funny book with serious things to say, *The Pyramid* belongs to an important tradition of comic social fiction, as the evocation of the spirit of Anthony Trollope is intended to make clear. But far from sharing in the sentiment and nostalgia which the twentieth century has read into Trollope, Golding's comic masterpiece is filled with laughter caused by discomforting awareness of the limitations and absurdities of life. The writing is witty, as the tradition demands, but the author risks destroying the delicate web of English social comedy by a number of astonishingly heavy jokes, which turn out to be part of a calculated shock he is administering to the form in order to brace it once more with a satisfying rigor of thought. In all his novels Golding embodies unresolvable complexities of existence in stories which are among the most mythopoeic of the century. In *The Pyramid* the complexities are there again, and this time Golding makes the difficult reconciliations of the comic fiction of English society with sharp, penetrating criticism, and of finely discriminating social perceptions with the downright dirty joke. It is remarkable that he could take a tradition so well established and use it for his own ends without falling victim to the nostalgia, sentimentality and intellectual softness that bedevil it, and instead, by playing on its conventions, produce a thoroughly antinostalgic and biting work.

In part *The Pyramid* is about the narrator, Oliver, growing up, and consists of three stories, interlocking in a complicated pattern.[1] The first section concerns Oliver's sexual initiation with Evie Babbacombe in 'the erotic woods'.[2] In the second, he overcomes his calf love for Imogen Grantley and brushes with transvestite homosexuality, which he does not understand. The final part is devoted to the longer process by which he emancipates himself from other crippling elements in his upbringing, especially a guilt-complex and the crushing influence of his music teacher, Miss Dawlish. This process is not completed until he is in his forties, a prosperous family man, but still needing to be protected from the world by 'the security of leather and steel and glass' of his car [p. 159].

The story of Oliver's early life is not merely related against a social background; a social field of force impinges on his every thought and deed. The problem of the individual's relation to society has always been a fruitful area of investigation for the novelist, and the doubts raised about the possibilities of free action connect with the concerns of Golding's other novels. *The Pyramid* in fact occupies an intersection of the interests of the earlier Golding with the great Victorians. Oliver is seen not as an individual simply acting with regard to those around him, but as one whose being is to an alarming degree determined by external pressures.

In the first place, the social distance between himself, the dispenser's son, and Evie, the town crier's daughter, is the key to his dealings with her and is expressed at the beginning by an elegantly simple 'of course we had never spoken. Never met. Obviously. . . .' [p. 13]. By virtue of her low status, Evie seems to Oliver to have an understanding and experience of the world which he lacks. He belongs to that insecure section of the lower middle class that is more deprived, in a social sense, than anyone else in Stilbourne. Just as obviously, the doctor's son, Bobby Ewan, who wanted to make Olly his slave when they were toddlers [p. 23], is socially out of Olly's range – the gulf exaggerated by Bobby's 'Duke of Wellington's profile' [p. 57]. Oliver can overcome Ewan's boarding-school superiority, but only by dirty fighting or low cunning, without regard for gentlemanly conventions – that is, by the sheer efficiency which later makes him successful in chemical-warfare research. Bobby Ewan, whose instinct for self-preservation is less dominant than Oliver's, enters the Royal Air Force as a fighter pilot.

Because of his insecure position Oliver has to assert himself and grasp at all the advantages he can with all his intellectual and sexual vigor. Yet as a successful man over forty-five, he remains bitter at the way the doctor's family patronised him: 'And ruefully I remember how the Ewans always gave me a present at Christmas. They also vibrated in time to the crystal pyramid' (p. 178). The social order controls everyone, and from the beginning Oliver, maimed by convention, is aware that his personal freedom is circumscribed.

The social workings of *The Pyramid* are more complicated than this, but to the alert reader the nuances are explained in the narrative. As so often in novels in which social relations play a large part, the novelist convinces us of the coherence of what he presents not by referring us outside his novel to some external truth, but by incorporating into his novel the rules by which his fictional society operates. In *The Pyramid* these rules are those obtaining in the world in which the contemporary reader lives, and the novel is in this sense realistic. The English reader feels a pleasure of recognition, but everything the reader needs to know is in the text, and one of Oliver's functions is to interpret otherwise cryptic social information.

To point up the Stilbourne hierarchy, there is emphasis on army ranks: Sergeant Babbacombe, Sergeant Major O'Donovan and Captain Wilmot. The whole question of Oliver's exact social level as the dispenser's son can be condensed into a hilarious dispute as to how he should be addressed when he plays the palace guard in *King of Hearts*. His mother will not have him called 'Sergeant', which would put him on a level with the Babbacombes, while 'Colonel' is too lofty. This dispute rages around a silent Oliver, and the final compromise of 'Captain' – reached without his consent – is an analogy of Oliver's whole social history.

In the third section, another sort of comedy is developed around the Stilbourne activity of watching neighbors and intuiting intimate details about their lives from their smallest movements. Life in Oliver's world is experienced at one remove from reality. Like other women of Stilbourne, Oliver's mother plays his game with consummate skill, not concealing her scorn for her menfolk when they fail to follow her logic. She has a social radar of her own and can use young Olly as 'a kind of interplanetary probe' [p. 177] – an inanimate tool to exploit without regard to his feelings about 'the unforeseeable perils of interplanetary travel' [p. 180], much as he will later exploit others. Incidentally, his mother is a great comic character, with her preternaturally acute perceptions and a style of delivery which defies mundane logic much as Mrs Nickleby's does.

Nothing said so far indicates that *The Pyramid* is more than good social comedy, with an eye to the psychological development of its protagonist. But this is a partial interpretation. What disturbs the mode of the novel is a series of dirty jokes almost too crude for the more subdued comedy in which they are set. One can instance Olly's father's preference for 'a *good grind*' on his violin [p. 140] or the nickname *Kummer* that Bounce uses for Oliver – eventually revealing the sexual significance of the name when she asks if he is looking for a girl in the woods. Jokes of this nature manifest the unstable aspects of the fictional world, which tends to erupt periodically into farcical hilarity with disturbing implications. For example, there is the way Bounce's car moves off almost under its own volition while Bobby Ewan and Evie are having sex in it, as a parallel to the way Henry Williams and his machines take over Stilbourne and, by implication, the world.

Again, Oliver's embarrassment at having to take his halberd through the auditorium during *King of Hearts* exemplifies man's inability to organise a secure existence in the face of the anarchy that threatens him. Olly, unable to get his weapon 'up the back passage' and advised to 'enter from in front', cries out a despairing, 'But they'll see me!' [p. 152]. This moment in the second section of the novel, paralleling Oliver's exposure to his father's binoculars while having intercourse with Evie in the first part, is one of the shattering experiences that disturb the placid, flat 'coloured picture of Stilbourne' and show the impossibility of security in the world. The three story-segments are punctuated by such traumatic moments, most of them involving the nakedness and exposure of Oliver or those around him. In these moments the harshness of life is laid bare, and the surface of social comedy is ripped open to reveal the alarming disorder that reigns underneath. Like the weals on Evie's backside from Captain Wilmot's beatings, these moments of violent awareness impress themselves on Oliver as though they were marks on the cosmos, radically contradicting the fundamental myths of Stilbourne society. Is not Miss Dawlish happy only when she goes out into the street without her clothes on?

Avril Henry has drawn up an impressive catalog of the varieties of sexual activity described or hinted at in *The Pyramid*, including incest, flagellation and transvestism.[3] But the shocks the author administers in the traumatic flashes are not on the level of newspaper scandal, from which Stilbourne gets its 'shocked purging' [p. 114]. Such revelations in *The News of the World* ultimately reinforce the status quo, but *The Pyramid* makes the reader aware of the deforming pressures of its fictional society. *The Pyramid* is necessarily unnostalgic, since life in Oliver's world cannot be imagined as ever being other than hard, dangerous, and destructive. When in the third part the narrator recounts his return to Stilbourne to confront his childhood and youth, nostalgia is inappropriate after the pain of the first two sections. The perfectly controlled relationship between Oliver as narrator and Oliver as a child can be compared to Dickens's mastery in *Great Expectations*, which is understood through the attitude of Mr Pirrip, the middle-aged narrator, to the young Pip. A fitting contrast is provided by the opposition set up by George Orwell in Bowling's return to Lower Binfield in *Coming Up for Air* – although Orwell's simpler nostalgic formula is justified by his polemic ends. The narrator's final awareness in *The Pyramid* has nothing to do with sentimental attachment to the past but is an understanding of self, when at last he recognises his own moral physiognomy in the face of Henry Williams, the archexploiter and evil genius of materialism.

The traumatic flashes in *The Pyramid* register themselves on the narrator's mind in much the same way as do Jocelin's in *The Spire*. It is this kind of indelible picture which Jocelin sees of the men having Pangall at the broom's end, while Goody Pangall, her dress torn, clutches the pillar behind her: the sight 'was printed on his eye for ever. Whenever there should be darkness and no thought, the picture would come back.'[4] A comparable picture for Oliver is Evie's face with its depth of hurt, 'make-up struck on a dead, white face', as she asks for tenderness and he responds with a Rabelaisian gesture. Such pictures 'burn themselves into the eye and can be examined ever after in minute detail' [p. 89]. Oliver explains the process when he describes a very early memory of Mr Dawlish smashing the Poor Man's phonograph:

Now you may wonder how, at the age of three, I knew these people, their names and provenance; but a child's retina is such a perfect recording machine that given the impulse of interest or excitement it takes an indelible snapshot. . . . I saw them numberless times later and compared them with the snapshot that lay in my head, and indeed, still lies there. I take the snapshot from whatever drawer it lies in and sort my impressions into two piles – one of primary, ignorant perceptions; the other a gradual sophistication which tells me the horseshoe was cooling, my own white shoes made of kid, and Mr Dawlish a thwarted man.   [pp. 164–5]

Nearly always in Golding we are presented with raw, uncomprehended experience, and the central movement in all his novels is from ignorant perceptions, through increasingly complex awareness, to understanding. The moments of perception are eddies set up in the flux of experience by hard obstacles which obtrude from below and belie the orderly flow of daily life.

The three story-segments interlock chronologically and are not defined principally in terms of the protagonist's psychological development. The long outer sections examine an ideal by which men might seem to seek to live – love in the first part and devotion to art (music in this case) in the last – and each demolishes a proposition or motto related to the apparent ideal. In the first, the 'Amor vincit omnia' of Chaucer's Prioress is debased through Olly's crude translation, 'Love beats everything' [p. 37], which shows its ironic significance when the weals from Captain Wilmot's beating are revealed on Evie's backside. 'Heaven is music', which Henry Williams inscribes on Bounce's monument, forms the ironic motto of the last part. It is discredited by the misery of Bounce's life, by the physical torture of the infant Oliver when he is twisted into the position necessary for violin-playing, and by the recurrent crack of Mr Dawlish's ruler across his daughter's knuckles. Oliver comes to realise that real music is elsewhere, so that hopeless exclusion is added to his other frustrations.

The short middle section, or scherzo, concerns the Stilbourne Operatic Society, whose initials are a cry for salvation that will never come. This part contains the major themes of the outer movements in hilarous compression. It could be called a burlesque of them were they not already presented in comedy that frequently bursts into farce. This middle section is not just a bridging passage, but an epitome of the rest of the novel – a small pyramid that forms the top of the large pyramid, part of the whole yet geometrically similar to it, completing it at a still higher level of high comedy.

The English comic social novel does not often discredit society so radically. There is usually a level at which the vision of the novel ceases to be out of accord with the ideals of society as constituted at present or at some future date, or as it may be supposed to have been in the past. Yet from *The Pyramid* it would be hard to extract a model of a satisfactory social system, past, present or future.

Golding based some of his earlier fiction in the demolition of certain propositions about human nature and life. In *Lord of the*

Flies, he announces his intention of discrediting the pious optimism of *The Coral Island* and to this end appropriates the names of Ballantyne's characters for ironic effect while underlining his message by reference to the title of the South Sea idyll near the beginning. At the end, the naval officer's 'Jolly good show. Like the Coral Island' is a savage twist in the tail. *The Coral Island* provides a kind of false standard against which Golding's modern fable is played, and the allusions to Ballantyne open up a path into the heart of the book. *The Pyramid*, too, has a set of negative allusions, as well as its three ironic mottoes, being full of glances at Trollope's *Chronicles of Barsetshire*. It may help interpretation of the relation of *The Pyramid* to comic social fiction to establish what part these Trollopean references play.

Although the name Stilbourne is not taken from Trollope's Barsetshire, Golding places it in the vicinity of Barchester, between the city and Omnium. (The latter name, so suitable for Golding's purposes, is taken from a Trollopean duke.) Although Barchester is mentioned fairly frequently, this does not seem important at first, and none of the action takes place there. Golding would not be the first novelist to rifle the *Chronicles* for a ready-made setting, furnished with a full set of associations and complete in all its geographical detail, but he is not really concerned with the county Trollope created. Instead, he builds up the topology of Stilbourne with meticulous care.

The Trollopean allusions, then, are not individually useful borrowings. But taken together, they provide a standard to which all of Stilbourne life is referred, and the effect is central to the scheme of *The Pyramid*. We tend to regard Barsetshire as an archetype of Victorian England; by showing what it has become over the years, Golding uses the contrast to emphasise the twentieth-century quality of his account of English life. *The Pyramid* was published in 1967, exactly one hundred years after *The Last Chronicle of Barset*, and the changes from Trollope's time to Golding's are seen in such minor shocks as buses plying to and from Barchester, and the motorway which runs through Barsetshire, while satellites are passing over Trollope's county and scanning it. Faced with such large-scale change, the reader is unlikely to assume that English country life is one unchanging idyll.

In less obvious form the allusions extend much further. Imogen Grantley, vain and empty and so much out of Olly's reach, is grandniece of a dean of Barchester, and a transformation of the proud, frigid Griselda Grantley, the archdeacon's daughter and the old bishop's granddaughter, who marries into the aristocracy. Mr De Tracy comes from the metropolis and has different standards from those of the inhabitants of Barsetshire, rather like the de Courcys in, say, *Doctor Thorne*, while Mr Harvey, the incumbent of Bumstead Episcopi and double-bass player for the Stilbourne Operatic Society, is a transmogrification of Septimus Harding, the warden of Hiram's Hospital and father-in-law to the Rector of Plumstead Episcopi.

These references are not cheap jokes; together they form an ironic comment on the world of Stilbourne. One almost suspects a suppressed Trollope-trollop pun underlying the first section of the novel, for the crude sexuality of modern Barsetshire translates Plumstead into Bumstead Episcopi. But the irony has another edge and reminds us that facile nostalgia for Trollope's world does not correspond to Victorian social realities or to the truth about Trollope's novels. Mr Harvey is buried under a load of hay, but his innocent prototype is crushed by political forces; Plumstead Episcopi displays a gross lack of spiritually, and the name as clearly indicates the misapplication of church funds as Bumstead does the abuse of the body. A widespread, false and cosy view of Trollope is the standard of reference behind *The Pyramid*, where the source of ironic contrast depends upon something essentially false – a nostalgia for a world that never existed.

The most significant mention of Barchester comes just before Olly has intercourse with Evie for the last time, while his father watches them. Olly emerges from the woods on his way to meet her: 'It was said you could see the very tip of Barchester Spire from the crest of Pentry Hill and I circled the whole thing, before I climbed to the top. But there was a blue distance where Barchester and its spire might be' [pp. 97–8]. Turning from the prospect that is reputed in Stilbourne myth to contain the cathedral but does not, he catches sight of Evie waiting for him, a tiny white speck in view of Stilbourne and the whole country round about. A spiritual focus is lacking in Olly's world, but a sexual one is easy to find. Similarly, the main social institution of Trollope's Barsetshire, the Church of England, and Barchester Cathedral, with its symbolic spire, are actually out of sight. And the different grades of clergy in Trollope are replaced by the almost spurious army ranks of *The Pyramid*.

This scene may contain a covert reference to Golding's *The Spire*; there, the spire is all-important and plays a part the eponym of *The Pyramid* certainly does not. In the earlier book, the spire is the central, focal symbol, providing the chief organising principle and physically structuring the fictional world as well. The title has a direct relevance to that novel at all levels but the relation between the body of *The Pyramid* and its title is not explicit but of problematic, allusive complexity. Avril Henry has investigated the possible meanings of the title and linked them to the complex time-structure of the novel. She concludes: 'The Pyramid refers to monument, metronome and crystal, all linked by similar shape and by their relation to Time whether gesturing against it, imposing it or simply enjoying it. Between them the three carry a wide range of connotations: social and religious oppressiveness and aspiration, ancient traditions and crippling conventions, regulating and destructive discipline, communication and detection.'[5] The pyramid of the title has no exact physical representative in the fictional world of Stilbourne, no obvious symbolic significance, and no clear role in the social structure. If the pyramid is Bounce's monument, or her metronome, it is only inexactly so. If it refers to the crystals used in time-keeping devices and in radar, this relation with the imagery of the novel is by no means realised in the novel, and the reference is, to say the least, oblique. Any significance which operates through the single mention of Henry Williams's possible Egyptian holiday or through the epigraph from the *Instructions of Ptah-hotep* is equally indirect. To take it as the social pyramid, on the other hand, is to respond accurately to a resonance in the title which harmonises with the rest of the work; but this depends on a significance which has to be imported by the reader himself.

So this wonderfully complex novel is not epitomised by its title. At some depth, such a complex of connotations as those listed by Avril Henry may well have a formative role in the book, but *The Pyramid* is significantly unlike *The Spire* in that it is not a working out of the meaning of its own title. The title stands at a remove from the body of the novel, vibrating sympathetically in response to the several aspects of it that Avril Henry enumerates. Novel and title are not to be united by a simple parallelism but stand in a complex, suggestive relationship that opens up as many questions as it solves. Things are not straightforward in Golding's fictional world.

Source: essay in Jack I. Biles & Robert O. Evans (eds), *William Golding: Some Critical Considerations* (Lexington, Ky, 1978), pp. 176–87.

NOTES

1. For a valuable examination of this and various other aspects of *The Pyramid*, see Avril Henry, 'William Golding: *The Pyramid*', *Southern Review: An Australian Journal of Literary Studies*, 3 (1968), pp. 5–31 [excerpted in this volume – Ed.]

2. *The Pyramid* (London, 1967). p. 46.

3. Henry, '*The Pyramid*', pp. 5–31.

4. *The Spire* (London, 1964), p. 90.

5. Henry, '*The Pyramid*', pp. 5–31.

SELECT BIBLIOGRAPHY

The following are recommended for further reading and consultation. Additional references will be found in the notes to the Introduction, to Part One ('Golding and the Reviewers') and to the essay on 'Golding's Sources' in Part Two.

Howard S. Babb, *The Novels of William Golding* (Columbus, Ohio, 1971).

Jack I. Biles & Robert O. Evans (eds), *William Golding: Some Critical Considerations* (Lexington, Kentucky, 1978). This symposium includes a very useful bibliography by Jack I. Biles.

J. H. Buckley, *Season of Youth: The Bildungsroman from Dickens to Golding* (Cambridge, Mass., 1974), pp. 269–79. Mainly on *Free Fall*.

C. B. Cox, *The Free Spirit* (London, 1963), pp. 172–84.

Bernard F. Dick, *William Golding* (New York, 1967).

Leighton Hodson, *William Golding* (Edinburgh, 1969).

Mark Kinkead-Weekes & Ian Gregor, *William Golding: A Critical Study* (London, 1967; revised and expanded edition, 1984). The best critical study to date.

William Nelson, *William Golding's 'Lord of the Flies': A Source Book* (New York, 1963).

Bernard S. Oldsey & Stanley Weintraub, *The Art of William Golding* (New York, 1965).

NOTES ON CONTRIBUTORS

C. B. Cox: Taylor Professor of English Literature in the University of Manchester, and co-founder and editor of the *Critical Quarterly*; his books include *The Free Spirit* (1963), *Joseph Conrad: The Modern Imagination* (1974), and the Casebooks on T. S. Eliot's *The Waste Land* (with A. P. Hinchliffe) and Conrad's *The Heart of Darkness, Nostromo* and *Under Western Eyes*.

JAMES GINDIN: Professor of English, University of Michigan, Ann Arbor; his publications include *Postwar British Fiction* (1962) and *Harvest of a Quiet Eye: The Novel of Compassion* (1971).

PETER GREEN: Critic, novelist and historian; his books include *Essays in Antiquity* (1960) and *The Year of Salamis* (1970).

IAN GREGOR: Professor of Modern English Literature, University of Kent; his books include *The Great Web: The Form of Hardy's Major Fiction* (1974) and (with Brian Nicholas) *The Moral and the Story* (1962).

AVRIL HENRY: Senior Lecturer in English Medieval Studies in the University of Exeter; apart from three essays on Golding, her publications are in the field of medieval literature and art.

SAMUEL HYNES: Professor of English, Princeton University; he has published *The Edwardian Turn of Mind* (1968), *The Auden Generation* (1976) and other books, and is the editor of the Oxford edition of *The Complete Poetical Works of Thomas Hardy* (1982–).

FRANK KERMODE: Fellow of King's College, Cambridge, and from 1974 to 1982 King Edward VII Professor of English Literature at Cambridge: his publications include *Romantic Image* (1957), *The Sense of an Ending* (1967) and *The Genesis of Secrecy* (1979).

MARK KINKEAD-WEEKES: Professor of English, University of Kent; his books include *Samuel Richardson: Dramatic Novelist* (1973).

SYLVÈRE MONOD: until his retirement he was Professor of English at the Sorbonne; his publications include *Dickens the Novelist* (1968) and translations and editions of Dickens.

NORMAN PAGE: for many years teaching in the English Department, University of Alberta, in 1985 he was appointed to a chair in English Studies, University of Nottingham; his books include *Thomas Hardy* (1977), *A. E. Housman: A Critical Biography* (1983) and the Casebooks on Dickens '*Hard Times*', '*Great Expectations*' & '*Our Mutual Friend*' and on *The Language of Literature*.

include *Thomas Hardy* (1977), *A. E. Housman: A Critical Biography* (1983), and the Casebooks on *Dickens: 'Hard Times', 'Great Expectations' and 'Our Mutual Friend'* and on *The Language of Literature.*

JOHN PETER: formerly Professor of English, University of Victoria; his publications include *Complaint and Satire in Early English Literature* (1956) and *A Critique of 'Paradise Lost'* (1970). He died in 1983.

V. S. PRITCHETT: novelist, short-story writer and critic; his critical writings include *The Living Novel and Later Appreciations* (1964), *The Myth Makers* (1979) and *The Tale Bearers* (1980).

DAVID SKILTON: Professor of English at St David's College, Lampeter; his books include *Anthony Trollope and his Contemporaries* (1972) and *The English Novel: Defoe to the Victorians* (1977).

ACKNOWLEDGEMENTS

The editor and publishers wish to thank the following who have kindly given permission for the use of copyright material: C B Cox, extract from an article 'Lord of the Flies' in Critical Quarterly 2 (1960) by permission of the author; James Gindin, extract from 'Gimmick' and 'Metaphor' in the novels of William Golding, in Modern Fiction Studies 6 (1960), reprinted with permission of the Purdue Research Foundation; William Golding, extracts from his novels, Lord of the Flies, Pincher Martin, The Inheritors, Free Fall, The Spire, The Pyramid by permission of Faber and Faber Ltd; Peter Green, extract from an essay 'The World of William Golding' in Transactions & Proceedings of the Royal Society of Literature 32 (1963), by permission of Oxford University Press; Avril Henry, extract from 'William Golding: The Pyramid' in Southern Review 3 (1968–9) by permission of the author; Samuel Hynes, extracts from the essay in Six Contemporary Novelists, edited by George Stade (1976), copyright and permission Columbia University Press; Frank Kermode, extract from Continuities (1968) by permission of A D Peters & Co Ltd; M Kinkead-Weekes & Ian Gregor, extract from 'William Golding: A Critical Study' (1967) by permission of Faber and Faber Ltd; Sylvia Monod, extract from an essay 'William Golding's View of the Human Condition in Free Fall' in The Uses of Fiction, edited by Douglas Jefferson and Graham Martin (1982) by permission of the Open University Enterprises Ltd; John Peter, extract from the essay 'The Fables of William Golding' published in The Kenyon Review XIX (1957). Copyright Kenyon College. Reprinted with the permission of Mrs Barbara Peter and Kenyon College; V S Pritchett, extract from an article 'Secret Parables' in the New Statesman 2.8.1958 by permission of the New Statesman; extract from Puzzles & Epiphanies (1962) by permission of Routledge & Kegan Paul plc; David Skilton, extract from 'Golding's The Spire' in Studies in Literary Imagination 2 (October 1969) extract from an essay 'The Pyramid and Comic Social Function' in William Golding: some critical considerations, edited by Jack I Biles and Robert O Evans (1978) by permission of The University Press of Kentucky.

Every effort has been made to trace all the copyright holders but if any have been inadvertently overlooked the publishers will be pleased to make the necessary arrangement at the first opportunity.

Index

Figures in **bold type** refer to main entries in the Selection.

Aeschylus 107
Aesop 100
Allen, Walter 22
Amis, Kingsley 12, 25
Arnold, Matthew 102
Austen, Jane 10, 102

Ballantyne, R. M. 37, 46, 48, 51, 54, 55–7, 80–1, 102–4, 106, 115, 146, 180
Beckett, Samuel 15
Bierce, Ambrose 106
Biles, Jack I. 27, 108
Blake, William 90
Boase, Alan M. 35
Brickner, Richard P. 29
Browning, Robert 108
Bryden, Ronald 25
Bunyan, John 11, 14, 103
Byatt, A. S. 166, 172
Byron, Lord 102

Camus, Albert 100, 107, 116, 135
Cervantes, Saavedra, Miguel de 101
Cocteau, Jean 35
Conrad, Joseph 14, 28, 52, 105, 106, 108, 138, 169
Corke, Hilary 25, 30
Cox, C. B. **115–21**
Crompton, D. W. 108

Dante 93
Darwin, Charles 105
Defoe, Daniel 11, 41, 46, 104, 107, 108, 130
Descartes, René 130

Dickens, Charles 14, 17, 104, 109, 141, 176, 178
Dorling, Taprell ('Taffrail') 106
Dostoievski, Feodor 16–17, 34

Eliot, George 14, 17
Eliot, T. S. 53, 54, 91, 101, 103

Falkner, J. Meade 108
Fielding, Henry 101
Forster, E. M. 23
Fraser, G. S. 23
Frazer, James 81
Freud, Sigmund 81
Furbank, P. N. 28, 101, 108

Garnett, Richard 88
Gindin, James 13, **66–75**
Golding, William, works of: *Brass Butterfly, The* 10, 50, 88–9, 92; *Darkness Visible* 10, 12, 13, 17, 102; *Envoy Extraordinary* 88–9, 92; *Free Fall* 8, 9, 11, 12, 13, 15–16, 26–7, 28, 50, 63–5, 72–4, 92–6, 107–8, 133–44; *Hot Gates, The* 10; *Inheritors, The* 8, 12, 14, 15, 23–4, 39–41, 44, 45, 47–8, 50, 52–3, 58–60, 69–70, 79, 85–8, 102, 105–6, 122–5, 133, 135, 138, 155; *Lord of the Flies* 8, 9, 10, 11, 13–14, 21–3, 28, 36–9, 40, 41, 42, 44, 46, 48–9, 50, 52, 54, 55–8, 60, 67–9, 74, 79, 80–5, 86, 98, 102–5, 115–21, 122, 125, 127, 128, 133, 134, 138; *Paper Men, The* 10, 12, 17, 30; *Pincher Martin* 8, 12, 14–15, 21, 24–6, 41–5, 48, 49–51,

Golding, William, works of –
    continued
    60–3, 70–2, 74, 79, 89–92, 98,
    106–7, 125–34, 135, 138; *Pyramid,
    The* 8, 10, 12, 13, 18, 29–30, 133,
    166–83; *Rites of Passage* 10, 13,
    110; *Scorpion God, The* 10; *Spire,
    The* 10, 13, 18, 27–9, 108, 133,
    138, 146–65
Gray, Thomas 101
Green, Peter 9, 24–5, **76–97**, 107
Gregor Ian and Kinkead-Weekes,
    Mark 65, 94, **122–5**, 134, 136,
    142

Halle, Louis J. 22–3
Hardy, Thomas 9, 17
Harvey, W. J. 26, 89–90, 92
Hawthorne, Nathaniel 14
Henry, Avril 17, 29, **166–73**, 182,
    183
Henry, O. 25
Heppenstall, Rayner 136–7
Hewitt, Douglas 22
Holst, Gustav 130
Homer 101, 103
Hopkins, G. M. 16
Hough, Graham 27
Hueffer, F. M. 106
Hughes, Richard 46, 48–9, 81,
    104, 108
Huxley, Aldous 86, 169
Hynes, Samuel **97–100**, **125–33**

Ibsen, Henrik 108, 159

James, Henry 14
Jennings, Elizabeth 29
Jones, David 53
Josipovici, Gabriel 107
Joyce, James 103, 107

Kafka, Frank 16, 35, 52, 100, 116,
    126
Kermode, Frank 9, 21, 23, 24, 26,
    27, 28, **50–66**, 85–6, 91, 96,
    146–51

Kinkead-Weekes, Mark: *see* Ian
    Gregor

Lawrence, D. H. 9, 17, 33–4, 57,
    107, 109
Lesage, A.-R. 101
Lodge, David 28

Mallarmé, Stéphane 65
Malraux, André 135
Marlowe, Christopher 90
Melville, Hermann 14
Metcalf, John 23
Miller, Arthur 169
Milton, John 11, 34, 64, 90, 101,
    103
Monod, Sylvère **133–44**
Moravia, Alberto 35
Murdoch, Iris 42, 116

Orwell, George 11, 33–4, 35, 107,
    178

Painter, George D. 23
Peter, John 9, **33–45**, 84, 89
Piaget, Jean 81
Poe, Edgar Allan 107, 126
Pritchett, V. S. **46–50**, 81

Quigley, Isabel 8, 24

Rees, Goronwy 26
Roberts, Michael 106
Ryan, J. S. 105

Sartre, Jean-Paul 90
Seymour-Smith, Martin 29–30
Shakespeare, William 14, 15, 22,
    34, 36, 110, 130, 144
Shelley, P. B. 107
Skilton, David 17, 29, 108,
    151–65, 173–83
Snow, C. P. 16
Southey, Robert 102
Spark, Muriel 104
Spenser, Edmund 11

Swift, Jonathan   11, 39, 40, 126

'Taffrail': *see* Dorling, Taprell
Talon, Henri A.   134, 139, 142
Tchaikovsky, P. I.   130
Tolstoi, Leo   34–5
Tourneur, Cyril   34
Tovey, Donald   45
Trilling, Lionel   23
Trollope, Anthony   16, 108, 173, 180–2

Vaughan Williams, Ralph   149–50
Virgil   101

Wagner, Richard   130
Walton, William   39, 45
Warner, Rex   35, 52
Waugh, Evelyn   11
Wells, H. G.   24, 29, 40, 51, 54, 58, 85, 86, 102, 105, 106, 107, 124, 146
Wilde, Oscar   136
Wilson, Angus   11–12, 45
Woolf, Virginia   17
Wordsworth, William   34
Wyss, J. R.   104

Yeats, W. B.   54, 65
Young, Wayland   25